MW00448706

Patrick A. Pete/UCAN Media Publishing
Email: patrick@patrickpete.com
http://www.patrickpete.com

Ordering Information:
Quantity sales. Special discounts are available on quantity purchases by corporations, associations, and others. For details, contact the "Special Sales Department" at the email address above.

Discover Your Gift: How To Know You Are A Gift And Discover The Hero Within/ Patrick A. Pete. —1st ed.
ISBN 978-1-7325283-2-1

DISCOVER YOUR GIFT

Discover Your Gift

KNOW YOUR ARE A GIFT AND UNLEASH THE HERO WITHIN

Patrick A. Pete

Washington, DC

Table of Contents

This book is dedicated to my cousin, Andrea Pete. A beautiful soul who was supremely gifted, but never realized it. The world is less brighter because you are not here with us. I love you and miss you Cuz' You were more like a sister to me.'

Rest In Peace Cuz'

To My Beautiful Wife, Gwendolyn Pete
Last but not least, my beautiful wife, Gwendolyn (Scott) Pete of New Bern, North Carolina. You are an expression of God's love to me even when I have, at times, not appreciated you as much as I should. I want to acknowledge how I could not have written this book or done anything else without you, the greatest of which was producing our daughter.

FOREWORD

There are times when circumstances don't allow us to see just how special and unique each of us really is. And, it's in those dark and uncertain times when we need to believe in ourselves like never before. My life is an open book. My choices early on had consequences. But, I never let them define me. I knew that I had a gift, and while there were a great many bumps and stumbles along the way, I never lost sight of that fact. Patrick's book, *"Discover Your Gift: How To Know You Are A Gift and Discover the Hero Within"* is one that I wish I'd had when I was a homeless teenager, walking the bitterly cold streets of a Detroit winter. He's right. We, each of us, is a gift. To ourselves first, then our families and then, the wider world. If you can't see your gift yet, you need to get this book. If you can see your gift but, don't know what to do next, you too need to get this book! How things begin has no bearing on how things end. It's the stuff that happens in-between that makes all the difference in the world. I'm a gift, Patrick is a gift, and you're a gift as well. If there's one book you need to get this year that will make a difference in how you see yourself and what you can do to improve the world around you, it's Patrick Pete's wonderfully affirming and life-changing work. Sometimes we all need someone to light the way ahead. Patrick's " Discover Your Gift" is one such light.

Eric Thomas, Ph.D.
Founder, Eric Thomas & Associates, LLC.

"To Thine Own Self Be True."
— WILLIAM SHAKESPEARE

DISCOVER YOUR GIFT

PREFACE

"Don't wish it was easier wish you were better. Don't wish for less problems wish for more skills. Don't wish for less challenges wish for more wisdom" - Jim Rohn

THE GREATEST JOURNEY IN LIFE, IS YOUR PURSUIT, TO DISCOVER THE TRUE YOU. It is this journey that sets you on the path to your calling, purpose and gift. Sadly, however, many people never experience this wonderful journey because they never set out on it. They are on a journey, but tragically not the one intended for them. They languish in situations they did not choose, doing jobs they do not love, existing but not being alive. Filling up life with activity, but not fulfillment. I too was faced with this quandary, but I chose to pursue this great journey. A quest aligned with my gift. I wrote this book to share this change in path with you in the hope that it can benefit you as much as it has me. My desire is that you will take the journey. The journey all of us must take to answer our calling, know our gift and ultimately fulfill our purpose. But first, let me share with you a little about myself and my life's journey.

My Early Years

My earliest memories felt perfect, but as is often the case, especially in the mind of a child, life is not always what it appears. At eight years old, my parents divorced. Shattering what I thought was a utopian existence. My behavior reflected this life upheaval in the form of me being suspended nearly every year of school afterwards. When I graduated from high school I ranked 279th out of 329 students. To say my childhood was chaotic would be an understatement. I was sent to live with my father because I had become unmanageable for my young mother. At fourteen, I ran away from my father's home to go back and live with my mother. While in college I went back to live with my father, then to my maternal grandparents' home, and finally to my paternal grandmother's home before joining the Navy. I was a rolling stone. I quit or was fired from most of my jobs as an adolescent. My family was beginning to grow weary of me. My life was headed in the wrong direction.

My Health

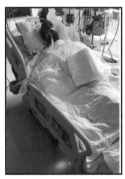

My health has been no cakewalk either. I have lived with Type 2 Diabetes for twenty-five years, I am a prostate cancer survivor, I have four stents in my coronary arteries, I've had two hernia surgeries, and quadruple bypass surgery. I am managing hypertension, I have hereditary high cholesterol, and a host of other health issues. As one anesthesiologist stated during one of my surgeries, "You got some bad genes!" I did not tell you that, however, to darken your day or seek pity. On the contrary, there were some extraordinary blessings and insights I gained during all of this. This is what I want to share.

Despite being the product of divorce, I am happily married after twenty-eight years. Despite coming from a bro-

6

ken home, I have successfully raised two children. Despite graduating in the bottom of my class in high school, at the age of forty, I graduated from college with a bachelor of science in Computer & Information Science. Despite being unable to maintain employment as a teenager, I served honorably in the US Navy for nearly ten years, and have managed to maintain a six-figure salary over the past twenty plus years as an IT professional. Despite my health challenges, I am still kicking, working out and fighting the good fight. What is my point?

All of my mistakes, failures, and poor decisions, combined with all of the struggles, trials and challenges, have not determined the ultimate direction and subsequent outcome of my life. To the contrary, they played a critical role in my success in life!

When most people experience adversities, they look at them as obstacles, as roadblocks in life. I prefer to view them as crossroads, forks in the road, as essential parts of the journey. A better word would be opportunities. A place where you become refined by adversity versus allowing yourself to be defined by it.

If you let bad life events define you, then your resume will read as a list of your mistakes, failures, and tragedies. You will be identified by your struggles, trials and challenges. When someone sees you, they will remember you for your mistakes, missteps, your lack of success. They will begin to identify you by what has happened to you versus the true you. This is a lie straight from the pit of hell! Make no mistake about it; What happens to you does not define you unless you allow it. Instead allow those experiences to do what they were intended to do; To make you and mold you into the best you, like the process of refining silver.

The refinement of silver, in many ways, is akin to experiencing adversity. When silver is subjected to heat at a certain temperature, it changes the state of the metal. It is in this change of state, the transformative phase, that something else also occurs. The impurities, which were previously a part of the precious metal, begin to separate. What it truly is separates from what it truly is not. This is the transformative power adversity brings into our lives. Like heat, adversity possesses the ability to put us in a state where what we truly are becomes separated from what we truly are not.

In refining silver, this is called the dross. This is what is skimmed of the top of molten silver. Truth be told, gold, diamonds and other precious stones are simply rocks until they have been dug up, processed and refined. This is because so many other things get intermingled with them between their creation and their discovery. The same goes for your true nature during the course of life. Before we go through the process of adversity, we look more like rocks than the precious jewels God created us to be. Have you ever heard how a silversmith knows when the silver has been sufficiently refined?

Earlier, we talked about the dross. The foreign matter in the molten metal. When the metal becomes heated to the right temperature, the dross rises to the top because the precious metal is of substance. It is heavier. The dross is not. The dross is waste, scum. When this occurs, the silversmith skims the dross from the molten metal. The silversmith keeps removing the dross until there is none left. How do they know they have removed all of the dross from the metal? They know this when they can see a clear reflection of themselves in the molten metal. True refinement occurs when you can see the true you.

The "True You"

While being refined is a process of transformation, it is also a process of discovery. Many miss this opportunity of discovery. They experience adversity and believe it reflects negatively upon them, when in reality it is how we respond to adversity that reveals our true nature. There are other benefits. When we know our true selves, we are in a position to hear and answer our calling. Our calling is what we are meant to do on this planet. We begin to understand our purpose, why we are called to execute our calling. Last but not least, our gift. Our gift is the unique power each of us possess which enables us to execute our calling. I call this the gifting trinity: our calling, our purpose and our gift. All of this from adversity. What many see as bad luck or a tough break is actually a great opportunity. If you can see this, I believe it will change your life. It changed mine. The world is so much better when we are better. My hope is that as you read this book, it will help you see just how much what you desire in your life is embedded in the struggles you experience.

Last but not least, adversity also brings us to a place of choosing the right path to take. The path that points you in the right direction in your journey. The path through which we experience our refinement. This is where you come to the crossroad, the decision point. The moment where you take the path that leads you to the true you versus the path that allows others to interpret you as they see fit, which ultimately results in a distortion of who you are truly.

No one except you and God play a role in how you are defined. In order for us to truly live the life we are destined to live, we must see ourselves in a true and authentic way. Without this we cannot discover the truth that God established when He created us. We are His gift to the world. Each and every human being was created to be a blessing to the world. As you will read in this book, there are reasons why this is, unfortunately, not always the outcome.

This is the great tragedy of life. I believe that if everyone were to know, master and operate in their gift, the world would be less violent, more peaceful and a better place. The reasons this is not the case are significant. We need to be aware of their treachery and minimize their impact. We must ensure that we are not one of those who do not fulfill their role as a gift to the world by not knowing, mastering, and operating in our gift.

This book, *"Discover Your Gift: How to Know You are a Gift and Unleash the Hero Within"* is the first of "The Gifted Life" book series. The second book is titled, *"Master Your Gift: Practical Steps to Being Your Hero"*. This second book focuses on the transformation, the specific actions and steps needed to master the true you, the gift that is you. The third book, titled *"Give Your Gift: The Hero in Action"*, deals with taking action and functioning in your true self. In other words, the act of impacting the world through operating in your gift.

Everyone is precious. EVERYONE! If only everyone realized this. My hope is this book will move the needle in that direction.

How To Read This Book

Finally, I want to express some things to the reader. This book is not simply a quick easy read. I ask that you take your time to digest the content of the book. While this book is not lengthy, I believe there is much depth to what is conveyed. There are a number of ideas and concepts that I present to you in this book. I pray I have done an adequate job in conveying them. To really gain a deep understanding of what you can get from this book, and the other books in the Gifted Life series, it will require you to look over some of the references, read the glossary, use the index and read the case studies provided in the appendix. It may require that you take some notes. Please read, think about, and answer the questions in each chapter. I believe this will make the content more effective for you from an application perspective. My ultimate hope is that this book sets in motion productive, thought-provoking discussion. Ask questions of yourself. Discuss the concepts in this book with others. Contact me and let's dialogue. With this collaboration, it is my belief this book will result in two things in your life.

First, the revelation about who you are and the beauty within you. Second, that you are motivated to act on that information and give yourself in a way that enriches you and all of us. The fact is we need you. You are a gift.

TRUTH

"THEN YOU WILL KNOW THE TRUTH AND THE TRUTH WILL SET YOU FREE"

THE BIBLE (MARK 8:32)

CHAPTER ONE

Can You Handle The Truth?

IF I WERE LIMITED TO MENTIONING ONE THING CRITICAL TO DISCOVERING YOUR GIFT, IT IS THE ABILITY TO EMBRACE TRUTH. As important as breathing is to living, so truth is to the revelation that you are a gift. An inability to accept and embrace truth is analogous to a person walking across a busy highway blindfolded. It may be possible to get across the road, but it is highly unlikely you will survive the journey.

Despite this seemingly simple reality, I have found that most don't welcome truth with open arms. This is especially the case when it comes to truth about themselves. We avoid it. In many cases, most are downright belligerent when presented with it. George R. R. Martin, the author of numerous best sellers and most notably the books series that inspired the TV series, Game of Thrones, sums it up best: "People often claim to hunger for truth, but seldom like the taste when it is served up."[26] Ironically, there is a paradox in this aversion to the truth. Deep down we know

---

26 "Quote by George R.R. Martin: "People often claim to hunger for truth ...." Accessed June 22, 2017. http://www.goodreads.com/quotes/415136-people-often-claim-to-hunger-for-truth-but-seldom-like.

the beauty of truth, because despite this dislike to the truth being applied to us, we require, no, demand it be presented to us with respect to others.

Truth is so important that our societies are built on it. You can be imprisoned in our society if you lie in court or to the government. Truth is central to order, structure, and integrity. The wonder of truth is so powerful that it inspires and motivates. When we embrace it, we are one step closer to spiritual wholeness. It is the spiritual carbon bonding that strengthens everything. Every religion supremely values it. Jesus, when describing Himself, says this, "I am the Way, the **Truth** and the Life."[27] So if truth is so self-evidently powerful, why then do people cower from it when it is applied to them? The answer is simple, pain. As the expression states, "The truth hurts." Indeed.

The Truth Hurts

Did you know that the brain does not differentiate between the pain you feel when you stub your toe and the pain you feel when faced with an unpleasant truth?[28] The same pain receptors fire off in your brain. When you stub your toe, your automatic response is to pull your toe back. We do the same when we are faced with unpleasant truths about ourselves. We avoid them. It is a neurological reflex. In order to know our true self, we must fight this natural response. To do otherwise severely limits our ability to identify truths about ourselves that we might not like but

27 "John 14:6 NKJV

28 Fogel, A. (2017). Emotional and Physical Pain Activate Similar Brain Regions. [online] Psychology Today. Available at: https://www.psychology-today.com/blog/body-sense/201204/emotional-and-physical-pain-activate-similarbrain-regions [Accessed 31 Aug. 2017].

are essential to discovering our true self. How can we know ourselves truly if we do not embrace everything, warts and all? Let me give you an example in marriage.

In marriage, knowing the good and the bad of each other and learning to embrace it is essential to experiencing true oneness as a couple. Likewise, knowing the true you involves embracing things about yourself that you might not like. Not addressing them prevents us from experiencing wholeness as a person, which is akin to oneness in marriage. This oneness/wholeness is the essence of true intimacy both in marriage and in knowing the true you. Closeness with your spouse to the degree that you know them, good and bad. Closeness with yourself that you know the true you, good and bad. This is the reason traditional wedding vows include the statement, "I promise to be true to you in good times and in bad, in sickness and in health." True intimacy is summarized in that statement. This is also an aspect of why many marriages fail. Most people say this statement, but when they experience the sickness, the bad times, or both, they naturally recoil. They experience a marital stubbing of their toe. Unfortunately, we do the same thing within ourselves. In marriage, this can result in divorce. The consequences as an individual are that a person can be out of touch with themselves. This can lead to a host of other issues, the least of which is the lack of success in one's endeavors; the worst could result in mental instability. We must fight this and desire to know ourselves in a deeper, more intimate way. This level of intimacy and knowing

> Deep physical intimacy is how we procreate. True soul intimacy with one's self produces a procreation of the soul. your Gift

oneself was not lost on the ancient Hebrews. For them, knowing and intimacy were, for all intents and purposes, one and the same.

In the Old Testament of the Bible, the Hebrew word 'yada' translated as "to know" and intimacy are used synonymously. In chapter four of the book of Genesis, it says that Adam knew Eve. He knew her in the sense of having become physically intimate with her. In other words, they had sexual intercourse. Now think about that for a minute. The word the writer chose to intimate (pun intended) sex is the same word that means "to know". Sex is the apex of physical intimacy. Likewise, you must reach that same level of intimacy with yourself from a soul perspective. Both physical sex and intimacy with oneself from a soul perspective requires a closeness that is so near it produces a procreative energy. Deep physical intimacy is how we procreate. It is what produces another human being. True soul intimacy with oneself produces a procreation of the soul.

Soul intimacy is procreative in the sense of producing the seeds of creation or ideas that results in the pregnancy of those ideas. This births your unique gift, and the fruits thereof. Just as a baby conceived by two parents produces a child that cannot be reproduced by any other combination of parents, your unique gift comes out of an inner intimacy that cannot be reproduced by others. It is unique to you. This, my friends, is one of the true blessings of knowing the true you. The blessing of having the inner intimacy that reproduces your ideas, thoughts, and gift to the world. Which if not birthed by you, leaves the world devoid of the gift that only you can produce to enrich it. This is what having a calling is really about. It is the genesis of the what.

It provides the motivation to be the true you, the fuel to be and do you. When you function in this space, you begin to see yourself in the beauty with which God sees you. You don't attempt to mimic others, because your intimacy with yourself allows you to truly see yourself for who you are. That person is beautiful. Not because of what others attempt to tell you about yourself, but because of what you have discovered from an authentic and genuine examination of yourself. I promise you, when you meet the true you, you will love that person. You must love yourself, if you are to be supremely effective in the lives of those you are called to impact. You cannot help others with maximum effect unless you love them and you can't love them if you don't first love yourself. Let's discuss the subject of loving yourself for a moment.

Love Yourself, but Don't Be In Love With Yourself

There are a number of books that spend an enormous amount of time trying to convince people that the world does not revolve around them. While it is important to emphasize that we should not think too much of ourselves, it does present a problem. The issue is there are a number of people who don't think much of themselves at all. The result is that while we are attempting to prevent egotistical self-centeredness, we unintentionally move the arrow past the proper

> Humility is the controlling rod to the power of Love

target. The result is we promote an environment where people begin to think less of themselves. Unfortunately for some, this results in depression and, in the worst case, can result in suicide. I believe the truth is somewhere in the middle. You are not the center of the universe, but you are a very important part of the universe. A part that without you would be incomplete and less than it could and should be. Let me express with more specificity what I mean when I say love yourself.

First, let's be clear, I am not talking about love in the sense of being a narcissist. That is the flip side of loving yourself; the evil twin if you will. Narcissism is really a mask for insecurity, which by definition is incongruent with your true self. Your true self needs no mask. In fact, the first thing you will do when you become your true self is discard the masks you wore. I won't stay here long, but I think telling you how we came up with the word narcissist will bring home this powerful point. Do you know the story in Greek mythology of Narcissus, from which the word narcissist is derived? I will not recount the whole story here, but hear is the gist of it.

Narcissus was so in love with himself that when he saw his reflection in a lake, he was so entranced by his own image he couldn't turn away from it. He lost the will to live and died staring at himself. What is the point? Love yourself, but do not be in love with yourself. Never mistake the two as the same.

What I would like you to focus on from this story is this. Narcissus' obsession with himself led to his destruction. If we are not careful we can become so obsessed with something or ourselves that our narcissism will destroy the very thing we obsess over. I could write an entire book on this subject alone, but I want to focus on how to love ourselves to the degree that it has maximum power without being overpowering. How do you do this? You should be humble. Humility is the controlling rod to the power of Love.

Humility is an interesting trait, because depending upon who you talk to, how it is defined can be demonstrably different. People use the word humble as a synonym for poor or lowly. This use of the word, while applicable, does somewhat of a disservice to it. Humility is much more than that. In fact, it is one of the most powerful postures we can have. Before I explain why, let's establish a definition for humility as it relates to our discussion. Humility is being mindful of your greatness while positioning yourself in a lower posture. Why is this important? Truth is best observed from a position of humility. Rarely can one know or even be exposed to truth from high on a hill. When we are in a position of power, we are not presented with truth from others. But when we are powerful and in a position of lowliness, we can both see truth and be empowered to act upon it. A great example of this is the reality TV show, Undercover Boss.

In this show, the boss disguises themselves as an employee in order to gain insights about their company. Let's think about this for a second. The boss needs to come into their company from a low-ranking position to garner real, authentic information about the company they run. Why? The reason is that position and power does not usually garner truth. Despots and dictators usually find this out the hard way. They usually are deposed because they are blinded by their position and the falsity of absolute power. Very rarely can someone find out what is truly going on from the position and power of the boss. People will tell you what you want to hear and only show you what they want you to see. Power and position, absent of humility, results in downfall. You have often heard it stated, "Pride goeth before the fall." This actually comes from a Biblical verse that also adds destruction into that equation.[29]

The end of the show usually results in the boss, the company and, in many cases, the employees, being changed for the better. I don't think it is a stretch to say that the bosses love their business. In many cases, they founded the company. It is their baby, but because of their love for the company and desire for it to get better, they humble themselves. That is the point. We must do the same within ourselves, and recognize that we are a boss in our life, story, and journey. We are the ones empowered to make changes in our lives, but we must approach it from a place of humility in order for it to be truly effective, truthful, and honest. If we do this, our love for ourselves will be true.

When you truly love something, you will do whatever you need to better it. This is true love. True love of oneself is unconditional love, which cannot be attained absent of truth. Truth is critical to success because without it, success becomes a moving target.

QUESTIONS TO ASK YOURSELF (CHAPTER 1):

DEFINE TRUTH IN YOUR OWN WORDS?

WHERE DO YOU SEE YOURSELF WITH RESPECT TO TRUTH?

DO YOU STRUGGLE WITH HUMILITY?

DO YOU SEE THE CORRELATION BETWEEN TRUTH, LOVE AND HUMILITY? IF SO, EXPLAIN.

------

29 Proverbs 16:18

Accountability
Honesty
Being Able to look in the mirror
not be blind to the truth
Starts w/ the Word of God
We build an idea of who we think we are

Being Intentional

CHAPTER TWO

The Importance of Truth To Your Success

"I don't think you can write, can't create anything without feeling right with the truth." - Quincy Jones[30]

IN THE PREVIOUS CHAPTER WE DISCUSSED TRUTH; DISCOVERING THE TRUE YOU, KNOWING YOUR CALLING, UNDERSTANDING YOUR PURPOSE, OPERATING IN YOUR GIFT, AND LOVING THAT PERSON. IN THIS CHAPTER, I WANT TO SPEAK IN MORE DETAIL ABOUT TRUTH'S CRITICALITY TO SUCCESS. The pursuit of success is in many ways analogous to climbing a mountain. Truth is the base camp for the climb to the peak of your success. When you get into a relationship, the relationship is made better because you enter into it grounded in truth. You can engage in a relationship with anyone and

> The most precious jewels of success do not come in pretty Tiffany jewelry boxes. They are usually packaged in dirty, grimy packages of criticism

30 An excerpt from the Netflix documentary, "QUINCY" ; R, Jones & A. Hicks; Motion picture on Online Streaming Service. (2018). United States: Netflix Original.

easily determine whether they are a complement to the true you or not. The likelihood of success in those relationships is increased when truth is a foundational principle within the relationship. When you execute a task, you can execute it with clarity and an effort that reflects you. It is far easier to do a thing well when what you are doing is aligned with the true you. When others want to weigh in on what you are doing or give their opinions, you have the ability to entertain them without embracing their opinions, being discouraged by them, and more importantly, not getting angry with them. I want to put a pin right here. One of the hidden jewels of embracing truth is the ability to benefit from criticism.

Quiet as it is kept, the most precious jewels of success do not come in pretty blue Tiffany jewelry boxes. On the contrary, they are usually packaged in dirty, grimy packages of criticism. Often, they are packaged in insults, barbs and jabs from those who seek to do you harm. More significantly, however, they can come from well-intentioned people who care about you. For these reasons, most people never get these jewels. They can't handle this griminess of criticism, even when it is constructive. Notice I didn't say like or love it. I said handle it. Not being able to handle criticism usually means you have to feel good about it before you will accept it. Your acceptance is determined by how it is said to you or how you feel at the moment. If you are in this crowd, more than likely your success will not be within your control, because the determining factor is based on things you can't control. If they say it right, you will accept it. If they say it wrong, you will miss the opportunity. This would be a tragedy. However, this is why the ability to embrace truth is so awesome!

When you function in truth, your vision is clearer. When someone states something in a manner you might not like, you will still be able to see the truth in what they say and benefit from it. You might still be in your feelings, but if you are someone who has mastered the ability to embrace truth, it will not blind you from seeing the jewel in the criticism. You will benefit regardless of what form the jewels of success are presented. Your ability to embrace truth will give you the opportunity to develop what I call "success awareness". In other words, you develop a cognitive skill to discern something that can be of benefit to your purpose, regardless of how it is presented. This increases your chances for success exponentially. As you begin to purposefully seek these jewels of success in criticism, you begin to see them more frequently, and then something amazing happens; you develop a skill of instantly noticing these jewels within criticism. Criticism is no longer a pain point, but a source of opportunity. This is a double blessing. Not only are you able to be blessed by criticism, but you are able to be self critical. This is powerful because no state is more transformative than being able to judge yourself. This magic is what transforms losers into winners, victims into victors, and second-place finishers into champions. Let me explain this differently to bring home this powerful point by expressing the science behind success and failure.

The Science of Success and Failure
"Winners Win and Losers Lose!" – Dr. Eric Thomas

Have you ever heard of "frequency illusion", also known as the Baader-Meinhof phenomenon?[31] Basically, this is a

---

31 Frequency illusion. (n.d.). Retrieved September 13, 2017, from https://rationalwiki.org/wiki/Frequency_illusion

neurological response that our brains perform when we experience something new. Our brains flag this through what is called "selective attention."[32] In other words, your brain begins to look for this new thing everywhere you go. Then you begin to feel as though you are seeing it more frequently. Your brain, then does something called "confirmation bias". It reaffirms this "frequency" by the number of times it sees this new thing, but this is not what is actually occurring. What is occurring is that once our brain flags this new thing, we begin to notice it more. It is a part of the pattern recognition aspect of our brains. Well guess what? We can use this same mechanism to train our brains to recognize these jewels of success in criticism more frequently. We develop a "success awareness", and over time begin to instinctively identify opportunities to succeed, and there you have it! This is the difference between winning and losing. Winners see opportunities to win because their minds are conditioned to identify opportunities to be successful. Whereas people who are conditioned to lose see opportunities to lose despite wanting to win. They are success blind. Amazing! This is the power of habit at work from a cognitive sense. One person is conditioned to notice opportunities to win and sees them, the other does the same inverse. It is that simple. Well, actually it is not, but you get the point.

There is a case study of Super Bowl 51 in the appendix of this book. It illustrates this in a way that shows it in a real-world scenario. My apologies to Atlanta Falcon fans in advance. None of this can happen, however, if we don't master the ability to embrace truth. In a nutshell, it is the critical ingredient to moving us from a losing mindset to

32 McLeod, S. A. (2008). Selective attention. Retrieved from www.simplypsychology.org/attention-models.html

a winner's mindset. We see things for what they are, not what we want them to be, or as we have identified in this chapter, what we have conditioned our minds to see.

Those who lose operate from a place of fear, which just happens to be closely related to lies. You may have heard it said that fear is an illusion, or the more familiar quoted statement by President Franklin Delano Roosevelt, "The only thing we have to fear is fear itself."[33] I absolutely believe this and have experienced the truth of this statement in my own life. Fear rarely comes from a place of truth. In fact, the more truth you operate in, the less fear you will experience. You will be able to clearly discern danger and avoid it. You will be able to identify whether a risk is a danger or an opportunity. This is an important ability when climbing the peak of your success. Pay close attention to this.

Truth, winning, and success are closely connected. Likewise, lies, losing, and failure are inextricably coupled. Truth and lies are points on the compass of life. The truth points toward your true north. Lies point you in the opposite direction.

Finally, truth allows you to develop core principles and values that are aligned with the true you, and not some other version of you. I want to call these true core values or principles. When adversity comes, and it will, if the principles you live by aren't true core values, the stresses that come with great pursuits will inevitably put a strain on you. This is just part of the game. I want to stress some-

---

33 "FDR's First Inaugural Address Declaring 'War' on the Great ...." Accessed June 22, 2017. https://www.archives.gov/education/lessons/fdr-inaugural.

thing here. Everyone has true core values. If you are in touch with them, they will anchor and provide stability to be and do anything. Just as many people aren't being their true selves, they aren't connected to their true core values, and subsequently aren't anchored by them. This is akin to the chain that connects a boat to its anchor. You can find yourself having set sail on a voyage ending at an unintended destination. Core values help keep you anchored to the true you. Let me use this example of a story from a TEDx talk, by Adam Leipzig[34] to illustrate the dangers of success without being anchored to true core values.

Adam Leipzig gave a TEDx talk where he discussed his 25th class reunion from Yale. He talked about how 80% of his classmates revealed they were unhappy with their lives. This was despite the fact they had become "successful" in the various endeavors in their lives. They were Ivy League graduates from one of the most prestigious universities in the world. They had gone on to accomplish many things in their respective fields. I don't think it would be presumptuous to say that they had become wealthy in the process. They had "achieved", yet while in reflection they were dissatisfied. That is what happens when your life's pursuits aren't anchored in your true core values and aligned with the true you. You pursue endeavors and accomplish them, only to find yourself experiencing feelings of lack and wanting. They leave you unsatisfied.

Dr. Stephen Covey, the author of the seminal book, "The 7 Habits of Highly Effective People", says it likes this, "If

---

34 Adam Leipzig Only Needs Five Minutes To Help You Find Your Life Purpose: https://tedxinnovations.ted.com/2016/05/16/adam-leipzig-only-needs-five-minutes-to-help-you-find-your-life-purpose

the ladder is not leaning against the right wall, every step we take just gets us to the wrong place faster!"[35] This is the danger of pursuit without being tethered to one's true core values. It becomes pursuit without purpose. This is the motivational and inspirational part of truth. With your true core values, you are empowered to be everything you can possibly be. How is that not inspirational and motivating? Without them, you are not empowered and aimless. That isn't even the worst outcome. The worst outcome occurs when not traveling your true path leads you down a path that leads to a perverted version of you. This is measured on what I call a YOU spectrum. The perverted you is the version that is on the wrong end of that spectrum. It is you at your worst. The true you is on the other end, the right end. You at your best. We will discuss this in more depth in the next chapter.?

Questions To Ask Yourself (Chapter 2):

How comfortable are you with truth?

Are you defensive when criticized?

One a scale of 1-10, how well do you critique yourself?

35 Covey, S. R. (1998). The 7 habits of Highly Effective People. p. 117, Provo, UT: Franklin Covey.

CHAPTER THREE

The True You Versus
The Perverted You

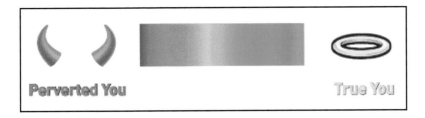

WHEN I INITIALLY STARTED WRITING THIS BOOK, I SHARED SOME OF THE CONCEPTS WITHIN IT. WHAT RESONATED THE MOST WITH PEOPLE IS THE NOTION OF A PERVERTED VERSION OF YOUR-SELF. I thought this was fascinating. I will explain what I believe is the reason why later. What is a perverted version of yourself? Put simply, a perverted version of you is the opposite end of being the true and authentic version of yourself. It is a false and inauthentic version of you. As I initially introduced in the previous chapter, we are on what I call a spectrum of self: the YOU spectrum. One end of this spectrum is the perverted you, with the true you at the opposite end. The majority of people are somewhere in the middle, not too unlike a bell curve. Those who do the most good in the world are in that small percentage of people on the YOU spectrum who know, be, and do their true selves to the fullest. Conversely, those who do the most evil are the people who are in the small group of individuals who embrace their perverted selves and subsequently unleash the most evil in the world. Let me give two examples to illustrate both the perverted and the true: Hitler and Jesus.

Hitler is arguably the evilest person of the modern era. His life unleashed suffering that is unparalleled, and yet when examined closely, Hitler was not without talents and abilities. He was an artist, a person who had an affinity for beauty in art and architecture. He clearly was a charismatic misleader, it is an affront to the word leader to call him that. The German people are a great people. You cannot misguide them unless your ability to mislead is extraordinary. He moved people. I believe this perverted version of Hitler was a gross disfiguring of who he was created to be. I do not believe that when God created Hitler, His intent was to create a monster, but this goes to the heart of perversion. According to many accounts of his upbringing, Hitler's life was one that distorted him. Early accounts of his life denote moments of struggle that were the turning points, the crossroads that ultimately determined the course of his life. The death of his mother. Hitler is said to have desired to be an artist and an architect. However, he was rejected by the premiere art school of the day in his native country, Austria, the Vienna Academy of Fine Arts.

Let us stop here for a moment because it highlights a very significant point. Hitler's upbringing and subsequent rejection of what was probably his purpose, that of an artist or architect, brought him to a crossroad in life, a fork in the road. His decision to take the path of destruction versus the path of his destiny ultimately led him to go from a distortion to a perversion of himself, subsequently plunging the entire world into war. Please do not miss this, because many times we believe that the choices we make about ourselves only impact ourselves. In the case of Hitler, it impacted the lives of millions and still reverberates to this day. Hitler, in effect, took a talent that was meant to be a gift to the world, and turned it into an instrument of terror. Now let us look at the life of Jesus.

For me, He is the very definition of a person operating in their gift, living out their true purpose and its subsequent impact on the world. There are many who will argue about the life of Jesus. Did He exist? Is He divine? I am not here to debate those questions, but few will argue with the impact of His life on the world. The extant information leaves little to no debate about this one thing: Jesus was a person whose life was good, and it was a life that positively impacted billions. The information we have available to us also provides a window into his early life. It gives us a picture of someone who had clarity of who He was. He then became that person and did what He was put on this Earth to do.

Jesus's upbringing was, from the very beginning, one that nurtured Him, both divinely and earthly, to know, be and do Him. He was His true self. As a result, we are all the better for it. This is at the heart of becoming the true you. You become a gift to the world. Jesus embodied this so much that a considerable portion of the spiritual world recognizes the blessings of Jesus's life, His true self. I want to point something out in these two contrasting examples. One life is consummately selfish. Hitler was consumed by his own twisted ideology. His book, Mein Kampf's title broadcasts it, "My Struggle". It is a diatribe of warped self-centeredness. The other life is consummately selfless. Everything about Jesus was about others. His magnus opus was the most selfless act one can do, giving His own life for the lives of others. This is a parallel and a paradox.

It is parallel in the sense that the more you understand who you are, the less you become concerned about yourself and what others think because you have an inner peace; a congruence of self. The paradox is you become more focused on sharing your gift with the world, your purpose. When you don't know who you are and operate in a distorted version of yourself, you cannot find solace or peace from within. So, you seek to attain it outwardly, usually at the expense of others. The more you truly know yourself, the more you are in touch with that part of you that God fashioned to be a blessing to the world. The truth is God creates us all to be a gift, which by definition is giving. The most divine characteristic of God is His spirit of giving. As a Christian, this is embodied in the following biblical verse, "For God so loved the world that He gave his only begotten Son . . ."[26] Knowing the true you compels you to give. This is the beautiful mystery of the true you. Once you become intimate with who you truly are, you want to share it. You want to give it to others. Conversely, the opposite is true when you are operating in a distortion of yourself. You are, in effect, lost. Masquerading as someone you feel you need to be versus being who you are called to be. The views that I am articulating, of course, are not made in a vacuum. These concepts of the true you versus a perverted you are a part of the

---

26 John 3:16 KJV

"great conversation"[27] about the true self versus the false self, first articulated by D. W. Winnicott[28].

D.W. Winnicott was a pediatrician and psychoanalyst who was most influential in the field of medicine called object relations theory. Object relations theory is an academic way of saying how we develop our psyche in relation to others during our childhood. In other words, how we see ourselves as we relate to those around us, especially during our formative years. His description of the true self is strikingly parallel to the true you. But the view of the false self, as Winnicott calls it, and the perverted you are strikingly different. Winnicott believes one comes into the world as a blank slate, that the environment around a person shapes and molds one's journey toward an authentic sense of self. The true you philosophy is similar, but not the same.

The difference is that the true you is divinely embedded in each and every one of us, the *Imago Dei*; the image of God. The Franciscan priest and bestselling author Richard Rohr's views are more closely aligned to the true you in that Father Rohr believes, as do I, that who we truly are was predestined by God. I, too, believe that we are all endowed with who we are called to be by God. It is hardwired into our mental, physical, and spiritual DNA. Our environment either promotes and nurtures it or distorts and, heaven forbid, perverts it. This is an important distinction because the attainment of an intimacy with the true you requires

27 Sindell, G. (2009). PRECEDENT: The Great Conversation. In The Genius Machine: The 11 Steps That Turn Raw Ideas Into Brilliance (p. 77). Novato, CA: New World Library.

28 Winnicott, D. W. (1988). The maturational process and the facilitating environment: Studies in the theory of emotional development. Madison, CT: International Universities Press.

that you realize, as Winnicott states, "the search for an authentic sense of self begins by looking on the inside." If your authentic search for the true you is attained externally, then the power of transformation is begun externally. This is a position of disempowerment.

When I say disempowerment I mean that as a human being we can no better determine what type of environment we will inhabit than we can predict the weather. We can only influence it. For example, we can influence the type of weather we will experience by moving to another place with a better climate. But even in those instances, the predictability of storms is even greater. Consider this, the weather in New Orleans is normally pretty good, but that didn't insulate that city from a storm that nearly destroyed the entire area. What we can do, however, is empower ourselves by finding ways to address the weather no matter where we live. This is the essence of empowerment. New Orleans wasn't changed forever because of Katrina. She was simply the catalyst. New Orleans was devastated because the city allowed the things it set in place to address weather anomalies, the levy system, to go into disrepair. When the storm hit, the levees failed and the city was nearly destroyed because of it. It wasn't the storm, but how the system was structured and then maintained that was the real issue.

Conversely, if our search for self is internal, then the transformation is internal. Your journey is like a city with a strong levy system. Anomalies will come, and they may slow you down but they won't stop you. Father Rohr, the author of the book, "The Immortal Diamond" weighs in on the dialogue of the true self versus the false self. The false self Father Rohr speaks of and the perverted version, or even distorted version of you are not the same. The false self, as Father Rohr defines it, relates to those things that may be a part of you. For example your job, school affiliation, and organizations you may participate in, such as a fraternity or sorority. We may use all of these to define ourselves. Another word for this might be the various masks we construct. The perverted or distorted version of you, however, is the result of external factors that adversely impact what you embrace and identify as yourself. They affect how you internally think of yourself. The mirror you place in front of you is one that is cracked and warped, but instead of seeing the mirror as the issue, we begin to believe the image we see as a true reflection of ourselves. We believe the lie as the truth. This ladies and gentlemen, is ground zero of the battle of the true you versus a distorted, or at its worst, a perverted you. This is a good time to discuss the correlation between the true you and the perverted you versus truth and lies.

There is a one to one parallel between the true you versus the perverted you and truth versus lies. If you are someone who embraces truth, the probability that you are connected with who you are truly is high, but if you are one who finds comfort in lies or half-truths, you are on the slippery slope of perversion.

In essence, if everything was stripped from you: your job, your roles, your accomplishments, your failures and your possessions, everything that has happened to you, what is left is the true you. This also applies to masks and untruths. When they are stripped away, you begin to see yourself for who you are truly. When you know the true you and love that person wholeheartedly, you will be in a divine space. This is who He sees when He looks at you.

The person He knew before the foundations of the Earth. The person God created to be a hero. But if you do like that person you will construct masks and untruths. This is not where you want to be. It blinds you to the hero within you.

The reality is you are a hero; a hero to others, but most importantly a hero to yourself. Can you remember life moments that were authentic and moments that were possibly distortions? If you can identify these and be able to make the distinction, you just may find yourself on the road of truly knowing your gift and discovering the hero within your hero's Journey.

Questions To Ask Yourself (Chapter 3):

On a scale from 1 to 10, 1 being a perverted version of you and 10 being the true you, where do you believe you are on the YOU spectrum?

What experiences do you feel have prevented you from becoming the true you?

What experiences do you feel have distorted you?

PATRICK PETE

CHAPTER FOUR

The TRUE YOU Journey; The Divine Quest

Discovering the Hero Within

THERE ARE VERY FEW PEOPLE I KNOW WHO DID NOT HAVE A HERO IN THEIR LIFE. HEROES, FOR MANY OF US, ARE ESSENTIAL HUMAN CONSTRUCTS. As social beings, heroes play a role in how we identify with ourselves, whether they are religious, social, political, or national. We seek them out. We gravitate to heroes or heroines we can identify with. Many countries national identities are defined by their heroes. The English hero is King Arthur. The Jewish hero is King David. Israel so identifies with King David that his symbol, the Star of David, is also the symbol for the entire nation of modern day Israel. You will not find many groups with an identity that does not have a hero as the central defining figure. As children, many of us find a hero and then attempt to place ourselves in that role. We role play as if we are the hero or heroine. Most of us have done it. Here is the problem. This places us in a situation where we can risk the danger of supplanting our true selves with this hero or heroine. This is an even more dangerous proposition when the hero or heroine is not someone we can identify with in any way except with the societal construct of that hero/heroine. Let me give you a personal example.

As an American Christian, all of the physical representations of Jesus Christ I saw growing up were of a blond-haired, blue-eyed Jesus. In my maternal grandparents' home, there was a picture of a blond, blue-eyed Jesus on one of those vintage tree slice art pictures. This was a disconnect for me. This was not a Jesus that I could identify with at all from a visual perspective, yet this was the image that was presented before me. Despite all of the things that were stated to me about this Jesus, this lingering question kept rearing its head in my mind, the proverbial eight hundred pound gorilla in the room. If I am made in the image of God, why does God not look like me? I could not get it out of my head. It bothered me. It almost caused me to stray from my Faith, but here was my saving grace. I had someone who did look like me, my grandfather, who was aligned with what I was reading and being taught about Jesus. The concepts of love, grace, and forgiveness came alive for me because the hero in my life, my grandfather, exemplified them. I could identify with him in a physical and familial way. This helped me make the spiritual connection. This evolved into a much larger revelation. There is no more deeply and divine a hero one can have than one's own self. You are anointed to be you, and as such are the greatest hero you can have. In every definition of a hero, you must be that person in your life. I have a number of people I look up to, and the one thing I see in all of them is the role of hero or heroine in their own story. Their journey to greatness was essentially a hero's journey.

The hero's journey is a great metaphor for the journey of life. This is the great journey mentioned in the preface of this book. We each begin our life on a journey, a quest. The American scholar, Jason Campbell, developed a pattern of literary narrative that outlines the various stages the hero goes through on their journey. It is remarkable how strikingly similar this journey is to life's journey.

These similarities, along with similarities within the life of Christ and a Jungian[26] exploration of self discovery, reveals a nexus between ones self journey and the hero's journey. The journey all humans have to take for discovery of themselves, the Jungian articulation of this journey from a psychoanalytical perspective, and the communal journey for identity best expressed by Joseph Campbell's hero journey. Let us explore Mr. Campbell's literary narrative, the hero's journey, in more depth.

In Joseph Campbell's hero journey, he lays out consistent moments that are a part of every hero's journey throughout history. There are a number of them (seventeen to be exact), but I want to hone in on seven that I believe are germane to what I want to call the hero's journey to the true you.

---

26 Jungian denotes anything that relates to the works of the Swiss psychologist and psychoanalyst Carl Jung. Dr. Jung primarily focused on how our thought, experiences and memories help shape our identity and personality.

They are:
- The Call: Your Assignment
- The Fear of the Call: Your Challenge
- The Coach: Your Guide
- The Gift: Your Offering to the World
- The Crossroad: The Moment of Decision
- The Test/Trial: The Revelation of the True You
- The Triumph: The Giving of Your Gift to the World

The Call – Your Assignment

"Many are called, but few are Chosen" – Matthew 22:14

No question distinguishes human beings from every other living creature more than the existential question of "What is my purpose?" and "Why am I here?" It is an ancient question that was probably being pondered in caves thousands of years ago. This question is really what has spawned religion, myths, belief in UFOs, gazing at the stars, the establishment of the "Search for Extraterrestrial Intelligence" (SETI) program, and a host of other attempts by humanity to grapple with this nagging uncertainty. While we exhaustively search externally for answers, there seems to be less endeavors to find answers to this question internally. This is not to say there are no endeavors to explore internally for answers to this question. The works of individuals in the field of psychology and psychoanalysis, such as Freud or in my research, the works of Carl Jung, explore this in an in-depth manner. In addition, there is no lack of books about finding your purpose in life. Books such as, *"The Purpose Driven Life"* by Pastor Rick Warren approach this question from a faith-based perspective. The popularity of all of the aforementioned works highlight one thing.

People want to know their purpose. It is with no surprise then, that the journey to the true you begins with this age-old question. Let's delve a little deeper into this part of the journey to the true you. What is the call, and what is your purpose?

The reason why the call and your purpose are intertwined is because the call is universal. There is a biblical verse that states, "For many are called, but few are chosen."[27] We will explore more about this verse when we discuss the "Fear of the Call", but here I want to focus on the "many are called" part of this verse. Everyone receives the call. Likewise, everyone has a purpose. The call, in effect, is what you are put on earth to do. Our purpose is the why. Our call is so intertwined with our purpose, that there is a duality in them. This duality provides depth to their meaning in the context of the true you journey. The call on our lives is not something that is inert, it is a live component of our existence. We think that because we do not know what it is, or have not recognized it, the call on our lives is simply sitting somewhere waiting to be discovered. No! The moment you were born it was activated. It has been beckoning you since birth. It has been calling you. We either answer the call or we do not. There is a reason why we do or don't. Let me explain in the best way I know how, through technology.

In IT, specifically networking, there are a number of reasons why a call does not connect. One reason could be interference. The call is made but noise makes the call unintelligible, or so weak that no communication can occur. Another reason could be the lack of a path. In other words, the call is made but there is no clear path between

27 Matthew 22:14 - KJV

the sender and the recipient. Let's look at both of these examples from a life perspective.

Many people's life situation creates an environment with so much noise that it prevents the connection to their calling from being heard. For example, you could have grown up in an underprivileged environment, you could have had an upbringing where you were hindered from your calling because of family dynamics, or you could have experienced a traumatic event that derailed you from following the path of your calling. All of this is noise and interference that for many does not allow them to hear the calling clearly. This applies to those who have an idea of what their calling may be. They are not sure, and in some cases, are completely mistaken about their calling all together. They end up doing something that does not provide the satisfaction which comes from truly knowing their calling and answering it. Then there are those who never get the call because the path is broken. This occurs when we are imprisoned. In other words, we have been placed, or have placed ourselves, in a state of incarceration. This could be spiritual, mental, or physical. While imprisoned, we cannot receive communication be-cause of restraints that have been placed on us in our lives, either by ourselves or others. These imprisonments are constructs of the mind. This includes physical imprison-ment. I am reminded of the noted psychoanalyst, Viktor Frankl's recounting of his ordeal of being in a Nazi death camp.

This story is recounted in his book about his experienc-es, "A Man's Search for Meaning" and in Stephen Covey's "The 7 Habits of Highly Effective People." The story ex-plains how he is in an environment designed for his de-struction. His entire family was killed with the exception of his sister, and yet as he recounts his experience in which this hell on earth becomes a place where he has an epiphany; he realizes that despite not having any control over his circumstance, he did have control over his response to it. His response was not to allow his dire circumstance to create something dire within himself. Instead he found meaning within himself in this hell. This is extraordinary, but really illustrates the point I want to make. The connection to our true selves can be lost. The path can be broken, but despite this there are still other paths we can follow. Frankl found the right path despite being in the wrong place.

I am not sure if you have heard this story, but Oprah Winfrey tells it as a way to guide those she leads. She recounts her grandmother hanging clothes on a line while growing up in rural Mississippi[28]. Oprah's grandmother turns back to Oprah, who was around four or five at the time, and says, *"Oprah Gail, you betta' watch me now 'cause one day you gon' have to learn how to do this for yo'self."* Despite this proclamation by her beloved gradnmother Oprah's says she said this to herself, "That's not gonna be my life!" What I want to focus on here was Oprah's hearing this voice despite the noise in her life. Growing up in segregationist, rural Mississippi in the 1950s, being the result of an unwanted pregnancy, and all that entails, she still heard that "still small voice" at five years old! Oprah attributes this voice to guiding her path to what we all know are Mt. Everest level heights.[29]

---

28 Winfrey, O. (2016, May), *Johnson C. Smith University 144th Commencement Speech*, presented at Johnson C. Smith University, Charlotte, NC.

29 There is a case study in the appendix of this book that goes into slightly more detail of this story told by Oprah Winfrey.

Both Oprah Winfrey and Viktor Frankl were able to find the paths to their calling despite the interference, the noise and the obstructions that we will inevitably experience in our lives. They possessed an awareness of these other paths. The beauty of their experiences is that they show that even in the most adverse situation, you can still discover your calling. Please indulge me with another IT analogy that I hope sheds more light on this point. Again, this will get a little technical, but please stay with me. I know you will be blessed by it.

One of the beauties of the Internet is its method of transmission for communication, the Transmission Control Protocol/Internet Protocol (TCP/IP). I won't get too much into the details, but basically when a piece of information leaves a computer using this protocol, there is a mode of communication that allows that information to reach its ultimate destination, regardless of whether the initial path of communication is broken. The information is fragmented and takes different paths, but ultimately will be reassembled at its destination. The reason for the creation of this transmission method was to develop a system of communication where, in the event of a nuclear strike, we could still communicate.[30]

In your life, you may experience a catastrophic event or live in a horrific environment that may impede your ability to connect with your true self. This does not mean that you cannot still make that connection to hear the call on

---

30 There is some dispute about this. Dr. Leonard Kleinrock one of the founding fathers of the Internet disputes this. He states that the purpose of the Internet was to facilitate resource sharing amongst researchers. With him being one of the fathers of the Internet I will not doubt him. I like the nuclear war version better, though.

your life. You must discover these other paths in order to receive the call. Viktor Frankl experienced the worst possible situation, and yet it refined him versus defined him. Actually, his trauma became the catalyst for his acceptance of the call on his life. He used it to bless others rather than allow it to destroy him, or even worse, make him a destroyer of others.

Juxtapose this against the response of Hitler. The question is how did this happen? Here is a man whose entire life was destroyed in an instant. His freedom and dignity robbed from him. I would find it hard to believe that he did not experience some fear. But as you read his book, it would seem that his fear, even in the midst of what most would consider the most horrific place in human existence, did not deter him from his calling. We know that Viktor Frankl went on to do greater things as a result of his horror. He used this horror as a catalyst rather than a calamity. To bring about the fulfillment of his calling. The reality is many people do not fulfill their calling because they fear it. They hear the call but do not answer it. Fear of the call causes many to refuse the call.

The Fear of the Call: Your Challenge

What prevents most from fulfilling their purpose? Fear. You are probably saying why would accepting one's calling be something to fear? Pain. Consider this, our calling and purpose is something that is hardcoded into us. There is a biblical verse that states God saying, "Before I formed you in the womb I

> **Nothing of true worth or value is attained without pain.**

knew you . . ."[31] Our calling and purpose are part and parcel of our very existence. Nothing is created simply for the sake of creation. Our calling and purpose is already known at that point. It is divine in nature. The path, however, from creation to fulfillment involves growth. Growth and pain are inextricably connected. Nothing of true worth or value is attained without pain. This is a lesson that is experienced from birth.

When we are born, it is a painful and traumatic experience for both the mother and child. When you work out to build a strong body, it is painful. You have heard it said, "No pain, no gain!" In chapter one we talked about pain being a critical factor in many people's inability to deal with truth. That same pain reflex causes us to refuse to accept the calling on our life. Let me use my life as an example.

For years I shied away from leadership. In my professional career, I wanted to do my own thing. I didn't want to take positions of leadership because I felt the burden of being responsible for others was too much. I didn't think I was worthy, nor did I have any inclination toward it. My upbringing was not one where I was groomed for it either. To be honest, the opposite was true. In many ways, my upbringing discouraged leadership. As a husband and father, I felt woefully inadequate. In addition, I had unrealistic desires. I wanted to be a singer, even though I couldn't sing, and an athlete. This only complicated the matter, but like a powerful river, sometimes life has a way of moving you in the direction of your destiny regardless, unless you fight against it and start paddling upstream against the current.

---

31 Jeremiah 1:5; New King James Version (NKJV)

This is what we do when we resist our calling. I call this "kicking against the goad"[32], a biblical term that describes when you are resisting something you cannot prevail over. You cannot win this battle. The longer you fight, the more tired you become and the more strength you lose. This also happens to be the telltale sign as to whether you are fighting to be who you are called to be or fighting against it. In the former, you gain strength from the battle, like a person who lifts weights gets stronger. In the latter, you lose strength. If you feel drained, whether it is your job, a relationship, whatever, you need to ask yourself, is this something I am supposed to be doing? Is it connected to who I truly am? Maybe you do not feel drained but tired. You don't dread what you are doing. You are simply exhausted. Maybe this is something that is aligned with your true self, but you just need rest. The old adage says it best, "Fatigue makes cowards of us all." We can become weary in the execution of our calling. You will see later in this book, that this is not because we are not being our true selves and doing what we should be doing. It is because we lack a guide and an understanding of what uniquely qualifies us to pursue our purpose, our gift. We end up wandering without direction. The guide is key to avoiding this. Two heads are better than one.

The Coach - Your Guide

The importance of having someone to help guide you in the pursuit of knowing the true you cannot be overstated. In fact, I would go so far as to say this is also hardwired in us. My hypothesis is that relational interaction promotes neurological growth. In other words, our brains grow in their capacity to learn through our interactions with oth-

---

32 Acts 26:14 - NJKV

ers. This is why a guide is so important. Let's use walking as an example.

How do children learn to walk? We are built to walk, physiologically. If I can go a step further, walking is a physical gift. That gift, however, is not manifested immediately. It is dormant in us. In other words, we do not come out of our mother's womb and immediately start walking. Babies, however, suckle automatically. The moment you put anything near their mouths they go to town. There is no need to coach them, nor do they need to perfect it. They are instant experts. Mammals that are born in the water automatically begin swimming. Winged insects are born instantly with the ability to fly. Walking, however, is promoted and nurtured through social and environmental interactions. We may even stumble upon walking, but it is nurturing and guidance that gets us to the point of mastery in a timely manner. Pursuit of the true you, although an innate pursuit, many times is derailed because one's environment does not foster and nurture the quest. It is like having the ability to walk, but being in a community of crawlers. Mastery of walking then becomes a crapshoot. Happenstance versus certainty. What you need is someone to stand up and walk as an example. What you need is a guide, a mentor, a coach.

I mentioned earlier about the need for someone to walk in the midst of crawlers in order for walking to begin. I want to focus on this, because there is a correlation between being an example and a guide. Simply having a guide is not enough. The odds of a crawler guiding you successfully toward walking is between slim and none. We can be motivated in an abstract manner, but we are built to see and do. This is why it is vitally important for whomever guides you on the journey toward the true you to have two things: operation of their true selves and familiarity with the journey you are about to take.

There is something powerful about aligning ourselves with those influencers who are in alignment with who we are truly. A much-quoted statement attributed to Albert Einstein says this, *"Everybody is a genius, but if you judge a fish by its ability to climb a tree, it will live its whole life believing that it is stupid."* It is not the fish that is the problem, it is what the fish is doing that is the problem. When looking for a mentor, what you cannot do is find a mentor who is a fish climbing a tree. You must find someone you can identify with who is operating in their gift. Now that you have found someone who you can identify with and who is operating in their gift, is that enough? The answer is no. Let me tell you why.

In chapter one, we talked about the importance of embracing the truth. There is no place where this is more important than in the person who is your guide. If you follow a guide who is not true to themselves, and to you, the risk is run of beginning the journey but never reaching the intended destination. Truth is the compass of the journey, and your guide, in many cases, holds that compass. If their compass is faulty, your journey may end in vain. Ensure that your guide's compass points true north.

There is one final responsibility of the guide that cannot be missed: The guide must have the ability to see within you, into your uniqueness, your gift. They must see the thing in you that distinguishes you. Again, this requires a level of truth within them that they can honestly see you for who you are truly. There is a level of spirituality involved in this attribute of the guide. In most cases your guide is a spiritual guide. Don't believe me? Let's look at some of the more familiar guides. King Arthur's guide was Merlin, who was a mystical guide. Within Jewish and Christian settings, the guide is almost always a prophet. For those of us who are geeks, the most famous guide or guides are the Jedi masters: Obi Wan Kenobi, and the much beloved Yoda. All of the aforementioned were guides to hero archetypes who did not yet know who they were. It was the guides who helped the heroes to realize things about themselves which were crucial to them becoming who they were truly. This is the beginning of self discovery. The guide sees it first but must have the ability to hold a mirror to the face of the hero so that they can see what the guide sees. How tragic would it be if the mirror they held up was dirty, scratched or warped? Or even worse, what if it was broken? I think I have made my point, but I left one thing out. The guide must be able to see the uniqueness in you, because within your uniqueness is that one thing you possess that no one else can replicate, your gift. There is a quote that says this, "When the student is ready, the teacher will appear."[33] When the guide appears, it will become clearer to you what your gift is because it is what attracted the guide to you. In other words, your gift will make room for you.

The Gift - Your Offering To The World

I want to again point to some well-known heroes, King Arthur, King David, and Luke Skywalker. Each of them possessed something unique that no one else possessed. It was this gift that revealed who they were truly. Men

---

33 This quote's origins are not definitive. It is ascribed to many ddifferent organizations primarily within Theosophical circles. As been ascribed to Buddhist circles, but this is not confirmed. In it's application here its inclusion in this book is within the context of the subject matter only

from all over the land attempted to pull Excalibur from the stone, but only King Arthur could pull the sword from the stone. King David was lined up with his brothers and, despite their resumes and talents, David was chosen. What revealed David's kingship was his slingshot. The moment he killed Goliath was when he was revealed as a true king. Luke Skywalker was sought out by his guide, Obi Wan Kenobi. His ability to be in tune with the Force drew his guide to him. What was symbolic of his gift was the light saber. These symbols—Excalibur, the slingshot, and the light saber—are representative of tools that are used to reveal the respective gift of each hero. The symbols are the instruments used to announce their uniqueness. They announce that there is something special about this person. This is the essence of the connection between the gift and the gifted. To be truthful, it is not the instruments themselves that are key. It is the situation where the instrument and the gifted meet—when the painter meets the canvas, the musician meets their instrument, the athlete walks into the sports arena. This is of the highest importance, because until then, often, the gifted are unaware of their gift. To them, they are nothing special. The moment the gifted discovers their gift is the moment their life changes and their world, no, the entire world, is forever altered. The course of human history is changed and altered in direct proportion to each individual, connecting to their gift or not. Sadly, it is a reality that many never become aware of the gift within them.

The powerful motivational speaker Les Brown said it best:

"The graveyard is the richest place on earth, because it is here that you will find all the hopes and dreams that were never fulfilled, the books that were never written,

the songs that were never sung, the inventions that were never shared, the cures that were never discovered, all because someone was too afraid to take that first step, keep with the problem, or determined to carry out their dream."[34]

A person's unawareness of their gift is analogous to a beached whale. A fish out of water. My prayer is that those who are on the beach of a dissatisfied, unfulfilled life move back out into the ocean of their destiny, swimming freely toward their purpose. Let me bring home this powerful point with a personal story.

My father, was, in my opinion, the most gifted person I have ever known. However, I do not believe he accomplished his purpose in life. As his child, I had a first hand, up close view of what that looked like. I know personally the impact of the gifted disconnecting from their gift. Before death was imminent for my father, what I remember most was the enormous amount of regret. A man that I saw cry few times in my life, cried practically every day in the last months, days and hours of his life. It left an indelible impression on me. Not operating in your gift is like seeing rust on a car and not doing anything about it. You feel discomfort in your life, but not painful enough to change. But here is the thing about rust, it is a slow, insidious destroyer. By the time you realize you should have done something, the damage will be irreversible. My father realized his mistakes in his dying days. It was too late. He had only reflection and regret left. Even worse you can go the path of Anakin Skywalker who knew his gift, but allowed it to be

---

34 "Quote by Les Brown: "The graveyard is the richest place on earth, be...".". http://www.goodreads.com/quotes/884712-the-graveyard-is-the-richest-place-on-earth-because-it. Accessed 5 Jun. 2017.

distorted by the trials and tribulations of life. When tested, he was unable to respond correctly. He came to a decision point in his life and failed to make the right choices. You also know him by another name, Darth Vader. This crossroad is the moment that one walks down the path of either becoming a hero or a villain in their lives, and the lives of others.

The Crossroad - The Moment of Decision

What truly determines the outcome of one's life is not what most think. It is not circumstance. It is not situation. It is not even opportunity. It is choice. Choice is the single most important factor in the direction of a person's life. This applies to any endeavor, but especially with respect to the hero's journey. One wrong choice can send you down a path that, at best, delays reaching your destination. At worst, it may leave you lost forever. Multiple bad choices may, at best, leave you lost. At worst, they may leave you not only at the end of your journey, but possibly the end of your life. This single piece of information, if embraced by the masses, would be earthshaking in its impact. Most people who make decisions that devastate their lives and the lives of others rarely make those decisions with a clear idea of the implications. One of my favorite Biblical verses says this, and I am paraphrasing:

> *"How does a man build a house without first considering the cost? For if he does so and is unable to finish is he not mocked by others?*[35]

This Biblical verse has within it a very profound truth. Each endeavor we embark on needs to be carefully thought

---

35 This is a paraphrasing of the biblical verse Luke 14:28

out. Likewise, in our quest for discovering our true selves, we will inevitably find ourselves at a number of decision points. Making these decisions could be an easy decision or it could be one gripped with fear, but make no mistake about it, these decisions will determine whether we live the life intended for us, or if we live the life assigned to us by others because we decided not to answer the call. This is where adversity plays another vital role in our journey. It is adversity that brings us face to face with the decision between the two paths. We talked about this in the preface, but I want to focus on its impact with respect to the journey.

The word *refine* means to improve or to go through a process. Actually, let's combine those two meanings into one. Refinement is going through the process of improvement. This is a core pillar of a truly successful life. Improving ourselves as a result of adversity. Conversely, being defined by adversity means that the adversity is determinative in identifying you. In effect, becoming your calling card. This is called the victim's mentality in many counseling circles. Here is a definition that I think is appropriate for our discussion: *"A Victim mentality is an acquired learned personality trait in which a person tends to regard themselves as a victim of the negative actions of others, and to behave as if this were the case even in the lack of clear evidence of such circumstances."*[36] Let's dissect this statement to bring home exactly what it means to be defined.

The first thing I want to highlight is this statement, "an acquired learned personality trait." The key is that when

36 The Victim Mentality - What it Is and Why You Have It. (2016, June 08). Retrieved November 11, 2017, from https://www.harleytherapy.co.uk/counselling/victim-mentality.htm

you fall into a victim's mentality it is not something that is innate. It is a learned activity. In other words, it is something that you acquired through the learning process. It is not truly you, but once you learn it, you are the initiator of this feeling. It is a decision you have made, a choice. The last statement of the aforementioned definition, says this, ". . . to behave as if this were the case even in the lack of clear evidence of such circumstances." In other words, when you allow yourself to be defined by what happens to you, a lie is being accepted and embraced as the truth by you. What it basically says is that the things that happen to you cannot define you unless you choose to allow them to do so. It is your acceptance of this label that gives it life, and nothing else. If you don't accept the label, it does not exist.

The question then arises, "Why do people allow themselves to be defined by what happens to them?" While being defined by what happens to you is the worst possible decision you can make, it is also the easiest one to make. Therein lies the paradox. When we come to our crossroad, the path to being defined versus refined is an enticing road. It is the easy road. It is the road most traveled because sadly, most people allow themselves to be defined versus refined. This has an added danger because we tend to gravitate to what the masses do. Conversely, the path of refinement is not an easy road. It very often is the path less traveled. It is the path with obstacles, thorns and thistles. That is because the path to your destiny will always be a path where you will be tested. Those who choose being refined must prove themselves worthy of the prize. Victory is not given, it is earned. This is a principle that everyone understands, but few embrace. The test is necessary because the only way to ensure that the true victor is worthy is for them to be tested. This is the only way to know.

The Test/Trial - The Revelation of The True You

I have always been fascinated by tests. I've always excelled at them. I am intrigued by the enormous amount of fear that grips many when they are faced with them. In fact, there is a clinical term for it, test anxiety. Most people struggle mightily with tests, but why? There are a number of theories. The answer is not simple. There are a number of factors involved. Some are related to physiological tendencies. In other words, some of us, myself for example, are high strung, whereas others are inclined to be calmer. There are some people who actually become physically ill when faced with tests. There are those who do what I would call over thinking. They think so much about the test that it creates a false narrative that the individual believes about the test. Tests are a struggle, but are essential for the journey.

We just discussed over thinking and creating a false narrative. This is synonymous with going on a journey with a broken compass. This is precarious because the reason for taking a test is to bring us to a place of refinement. We cannot get there with a broken compass. In effect, test anxiety has the same impact on the journey as a lack of truth. It is a construct of fear, and fear by its very nature is a lie. The core purpose of the journey is not the journey itself, nor is the final destination. The true value is the transformation of you while you are on the journey. There is no place where this is revealed more vividly than through the trials and tests you encounter while on the journey. If you traffic in fear, in any variation, you run the risk of failing the test. Not because you do not possess the ability to pass it, but because a mindset that is fearful short circuits your abilities.

I mentioned the struggles and trials that many people encounter when faced with tests. These tests are usually academic in nature, but the same anxieties exist when we go through any test or trial. For the purposes of this book, we will focus on the anxiety of tests in the form of adversity. Every adversity we experience and every trial we go through is a test. Just as a test is given to reveal your level of knowledge in an academic area, tests of adversity reveal the true you. Your response is the determining factor.

An often-stated quote attributed to the great Vince Lombardi says this, *"Adversity doesn't build character, it reveals it!"*[37] Normally within the construct of a journey, we believe that tests and trials are singular in nature. I do not believe this to be the case. I believe we experience a series of tests. For example, when we come to the aforementioned crossroad, that is a test. Tests reveal both heroes and villains. Let's look at the example of Hitler. He was faced with a decision point, a crossroad. He applied to the Academy of Fine Arts and the School of Architecture. What was his test? Rejection. What was his response?

I will let the words of author Steven Pressfield in his book, The War of Art articulate it best. *"It was easier for Hitler to start World War II than for him to face a blank*

37 "Does Adversity Build Character Or Reveal It Life Science Leader."
12 Jun. 2015, http://www.lifescienceleader.com/doc/does-adversity-buildcharacter-or-reveal-it-0001. Accessed 5 Jun. 2017.

square of canvas."[38] Hitler became the quintessential human manifestation of evil based on a bad decision made at a crossroad in his life. The moment of truth relative to his gift. This is important because often, when we are tested relative to our gift, we question ourselves. Do not do this. Hitler did this and millions of people were killed and the world plunged into a global war, the effects of which still reverberate today.

Rarely is the right path the easy path. Usually the converse is true. Let's look at Jesus of Nazareth, arguably the most loved human being to ever live. He too found Himself at a crossroad, a decision point. While in the Garden of Gethsemane and faced with the enormity of His Calling, He asks God to remove the burden of His Calling from Him. His response? Nevertheless, not my will but thy will be done. He was crucified shortly thereafter. There are two key things to point out in both stories. How we respond to the test when we are faced with that all important decision at the crossroad makes all the difference. In both cases, the potential impacts were polar opposites. For Hitler, it resulted in millions being killed and the world being plunged into war. In the case of Jesus, millions, if not billions, were exposed to a form of selfless love. When faced with the decision point, it is important to understand the implications of that decision. Who does it impact? Will it make the world a better place? I know this sounds counter intuitive. You are making a personal decision, but in doing so you should think about its external implications. Yes, that is exactly what I am saying.

---

38 Pressfield, S. (n.d.). The Unlived Life. In The War of Art: Break Through the Blocks and Win Your Inner Creative Battles (Kindle ver. 1.25.2; pp. Location-117). New York, NY: Black Irish Entertainment, LLC

In the book, The Genius Machine – The 11 Steps That Turn Raw Ideas into Brilliance by Gerald Sindell, one of the steps is entitled "Implications." In this step, Sindell challenges us to think about how our ideas will impact others. The chapter begins with a great quote,

"A genius thinker knows that nothing exists in a moral vacuum."[39]

When we come up with ideas, part of taking that idea and turning it into brilliance is knowing the implications on the lives of others. This is where most human beings make their biggest mistakes in making decisions about their lives. They think individualistically. They believe they have a right to make a decision without any concern for its implication on others. This, however, introduces the key ingredient for true evil, selfishness. Most religions, in some form or fashion, attempts to move its followers away from selfishness to selflessness. Let's use cancer to illustrate this point.

What truly defines cancer is that, at a cellular level, it behaves disruptively within the body. A cell that goes cancerous is not dangerous simply because it is cancerous. It is dangerous because it operates counter intuitively to its purpose within the body. It is a cell whose genetic instruction has been corrupted to the degree that it does not do what it is called to do, it does what it wants to do. This cellular disobedience ultimately destroys the body if not removed. Likewise, when we are faced with our test, central to our decision should be the implication of our decisions on others. When you make individual decisions devoid of any

39 Sindell, G. S. (2009). The Genius Machine: the 11 steps that turn raw ideas into brilliance. Novato, CA: New World Library. (Rohr, 2013)

idea of what the implications are to others, you introduce cancerous characteristics into the outcome of your decision. This results in dire consequences for you and for us all. Let's go back to the polar opposite examples of Hitler and Jesus. Both faced the crossroad of their journey to ultimately fulfilling or not fulfilling their calling. One chose selfishly, responding to rejection in such a way that it may have implanted within him a selfishness to insulate himself from the pain of rejection. When you encounter this, it should serve as a red flag. The response to pain inflicted should never be retribution. I can never truly know, but I believe that the pain of rejection may have been the catalyst that caused Hitler to walk down the wrong path. So, what should have been his response? Let us look at Jesus.

Jesus's response was opposite of Hitler's. His moment was in the Garden of Gethsemane. He responded not by saving his life, but by sacrificing it, even for those who sought to do him harm, and ultimately betrayed him. His defining act was one of ultimate sacrifice. "Greater love hath no man than to lay down his life for another."[40]

This is why knowing the true you is of vital importance. If you make this choice before you know who you truly are, or even worse, if you make this decision after having experienced a distorted life, the result will end in defeat. One final point to make about the test, it is not a closed book test. It is an open book test. Your guide and your gift are crucial to passing the test, to overcoming the trial. Many fail because they encounter their test or trial either without a guide or without their gift. Here is a faithful saying. *"Stir up the gift that is within you . . . God has not given us a spirit*

---

40 John 15:13 - King James Version (KJV)

of fear, but of power, love and a sound mind."[41] When we are faced with a test or trial, it is our gift that will make room for us. Our guide will shine a light on our gift. But we will also experience opposition. Opposition is part of the test. There are other interpretations that state we should fan the flames of the gift in us. Fear not, however, but function in the power and confidence of your gift, a love for those for whom your gift is meant, and a mastering of your gift. When you do this, triumph will then not be something we hope for, but something that is inevitable.

The Triumph - The Giving of Your Gift to The World

In our quest for knowing the True You, there is no completion to that journey unless that journey results in us reaching our intended destination. In the case of re-discovering the true you, triumph is in that rediscovery. Coming face to face with who you are truly. The truth is, this is a journey of self-discovery, but its end is not. The true triumph is not the rediscovery alone. It is also in the connection between this self-discovery and the gift. Consider the following examples: King Arthur and Excalibur, King David and his slingshot, Luke Skywalker and his light saber. This is the real prize. There is a symbiosis. The gift in the hands of the gifted helps them discover themselves. The gift never really serves its true purpose, or dare I say, discovers itself, until it is in the hands of the gifted. Let's look at the story of Excalibur in more depth.

While there are numerous variations on Excalibur's meaning, what I want to focus in on is that it identified King

---

41 2 Timothy 1:6-7 - New King James Version (NKJV)

Arthur's kingship. It revealed his royalty. It could only be pulled from the stone by the "Chosen One". We would not even know of the existence of Excalibur absent of its role in revealing the true king. Its immortality as a sword is cemented by its role in this revelation. We all have a royal role to play in this world. We and our gifts are central to this role. When they come together it becomes magical. It not only reveals our royal role, but it also reveals our character. What separates us from everyone else. Let's look at King David.

In the story of King David, the connection between the gifted and the symbolism in the gift are expressed beautifully. In the case of King David, the slingshot symbolizes the gift within. What does it reveal about King David? Without getting into the larger theological implications, the slingshot symbolizes that it is what's inside David that empowers his giant-slaying ability, not the tool he uses to do it. Consider the juxtaposition of the reigning King Saul's stature and massive armor, versus David's youth, diminutive size, and the slingshot. When faced with the giant, Goliath, it is not size that defeats him, but the confidence and faith in God that David possessed. His gift was his relationship with God. The slingshot and the battle with Goliath simply revealed it. This revelation of character really is what creates the attraction that inevitably occurs when we come to this place of triumph. When we begin entering into the triumphant part of the journey, the moment that defines triumph is what we do with the gift once we understand who we are and what is our gift. It is the giving of the gift that ultimately defines true triumph. This is the moment when self discovery and discovery of the gift are aligned. This gift alignment is the essence of triumph, because everyone, you, God, and those called to be blessed by your gift, all experience fulfillment. Let's look at another example, Luke Skywalker.

The story of Luke Skywalker embodies what takes place when the gift alignment occurs as well as its impact. The entire essence of the story of Star Wars is really about misalignment or imbalance. It is a tale about the forces of good searching for Luke in an effort to bring balance to the Force. When we don't know our true selves, and subsequently aren't operating in our gift, we are out of balance on a micro level. Once you reach the macro level, the world is out of balance. There is no research to validate this, but if there were I wouldn't be surprised if we could make a direct correlation to the state of the world as a whole and the state of individuals who do not know themselves and aren't operating in their gift. This would be a worldwide harmonic dissonance, like an orchestra of musicians playing the wrong instruments. Can you imagine what that would sound like? Musicians who not only did not know how to play the instruments they were playing, but subsequently could not play them well together. It is noise. Let's get back to the story of Luke Skywalker.

I am not sure how well you know the Star Wars anthology, but as someone whose entire life is bookmarked by it, I will give you an abbreviated version, highlighting the parts that summarize its role in understanding how triumph is ultimately achieved when there is interdependent harmony.

Luke is on the desert planet of Tatooine. He is discovered by his guide, Obi Wan Kenobi, who by the way is in search of something. What is he in search of? The one who is strong in the Force. There is an imbalance in the Force. All the while Luke is completely unaware of this. It is his subsequent journey that reveals all of this. He finds out who he is, his gift, and his purpose. He is royalty. What is his gift? He is strong in the Force and the lightsaber is the tool that helps reveal this fact. But what is his purpose? It is ultimately revealed. He is to bring harmony to the universe. None of this means anything if he doesn't ultimately destroy the Death Star and redeem his father. The scene where everyone celebrates on the forest moon Endor visualizes, in a cinematic way, true triumph. Triumph on the journey for the true you is the moment when the hero within you, the Luke Skywalker in you, fulfills their purpose and brings balance to your personal universe, which in turn moves the universe as a whole closer to its balance. The moment where the true you, the Jedi in you, is victorious over the perverted you, your Darth Vader.

We have talked about this journey, but have only skimmed the surface of the hero. Let's explore this archetype, because in the end it is this person who ultimately fulfills all of the above. When we discover the true you, what we find is the hero within us all.

Questions To Ask Yourself (Chapter 4):

Do you see yourself on the Hero's journey? If yes, where do you feel you are at on the journey? If no, why not?

What experiences do you feel have prevented you from becoming your True Self?

Do you have a coach or a guide? If so, who? If not, why?

The Hero In Action

THE TRUE YOU IN ACTION

CHAPTER FIVE

Who Are You? - The Hero in Action

I WANT TO GO BACK TO A QUOTE I MENTIONED EARLIER ATTRIBUTED TO ALBERT EINSTEIN,

"Everyone is a genius. But if you judge a fish by its ability to climb a tree, it will live its whole life believing that it is stupid."[26]

As you can tell by my repeated references, I love this quote! The beauty in it is that the genius in the fish is always there. But if someone walked by and saw the fish climbing a tree, they instantly would see the absurdity in the scene. The fish, however, does not see it. As crazy as this looks, the truth is the world is filled with tree-climbing fish. People engaged in activities that are not what they are created for, nor are they equipped for, but for whatever reason are locked into this routine of futility. Like the fish climbing the tree, they don't even know how absurd it looks. They just know it doesn't feel right. It feels stupid. They are dissatisfied, unfulfilled. The goal then is to get them to see that what they are doing is not as it should be.

---

22 "Everybody is a Genius. But If You Judge a Fish by Its Ability to Climb a ...." Accessed June 2, 2017. http://quoteinvestigator.com/2013/04/06/fish-climb/.

When we are placed in the right environment. When the fish is placed in its body of water, it doesn't float aimlessly. Immediately, they begin to swim. It instantly gets it! The gift is revealed. The same goes for us. What is so insidious about the tree-climbing fish is that if the only thing the fish knows are trees, they will live their lives believing they are a monkey or whatever other tree climbing species they find themselves amongst. In some extreme cases, they will even reject their own natural environment, all the while gasping for air in an environment that is not suited for them. The universal application of this quote can also be used to reveal a fundamental truth. There is a hero within us all. In the same way the fish struggles with climbing the tree, many of us languish in situations where we are heroes being cast as villains. When you discover the true you, the hero within, it is like a fish plucked from a tree and placed in their body of water. Notice I didn't say "a" body of water. There is a body of water, an environment that is uniquely tailored for you. Knowing who you are is all about finding that body of water. King Arthur found his kingdom and King David found his throne. When you find the hero within, you will find your body of water, your kingdom. Chapter 4 gave us a hint as to what path we must take to discover that hero. But in this chapter, we will get clarity about the path we take once we have discovered our true selves, our hero. Let's use Superman as an example of how your position is key to realizing your gift, and in the case of Superman, his superpower.

Superman is from the planet Krypton. Due to the impending doom of the planet, Superman's father, Jor-El devised a plan to send his baby son, whose name was Kal-El at the time, toward the planet Earth before Krypton exploded. Often, in order for your destiny to manifest, your past has to be blown up. Let that sink in for a minute. I am not sure if you know the story of Superman, but the gist of his story is that when he landed on Earth he possessed super-human power. As the leading scientist on Krypton, Jor-El knew that his son would possess superhuman powers on Earth. Kal-El's destiny was set in motion by his circumstances and his father's wisdom. It was predestined, but it was only when he landed on Earth that Kal-El's true destiny was revealed. This Superman story is so rich. Superman had three different identities. There is an evolution to his name. First, Kal-El, the name given to him by his family at birth, becomes Clark Kent when he comes to Earth. Then, his name becomes Superman. Let's walk through this evolution of names.

Superman's birth name was Kal-El. This name revealed much of what you needed to know about him. It describes to whom he was genetically connected. It described where he was from. It also gave some insight into why he was super. But as Kal-El lives his life, he goes from Kal-El to Clark Kent. I want to focus on this name for a minute, because many people are in the Clark Kent stage. This is the name they answer to but not the name that reflects their true selves. Clark Kent is a false name. A false identity. In a similar way, this story is true for all of us. You may or may not be who you are truly. And depending on a variety of circumstances, your name may not reflect your true identity. It is our responsibility to avoid getting stuck in the quicksand that is the Clark Kent stage of identity. While Kal-El is his birth name and reveals much about Superman, it lacks one thing. An indication as to what his calling, purpose and gift is to the world, his superpower. We know him as Superman, and we know his gift. He is faster than a speeding bullet, more powerful than a locomotive, and able to leap tall buildings in a single bound. He's Superman. The Man of Steel. It is his calling card. Calling card is a good way to describe the aforementioned statements about Kal-El, also known as, Superman because they reflect the critical aspects of our triple gifting, or in the case of Superman, his superpower. They all relate to how our existence is intrinsically connected to the way we will impact the world.

Superman's calling card does not reflect what he says about himself, but more what those he impacts think of him. Here is the great paradox with respect to our calling, purpose, and gifting. Superman must know who he is in order to be who he is. But the true indication that he is operating in his gift, his superpower, is when his gifting is reflected in the way those who he is called to impact identify him. Superman is derived from what those who receive the benefit of his superpower call him. This is the gift archetype, when our intimacy with our true selves coalesces with the transformative change we have on those we are called to impact.

Questions To Ask Yourself (Chapter 5):

Are you in a Clark Kent phase or Superman phase? If so, explain?

Write down what you feel your unique environment looks like?

PATRICK PETE

CHAPTER SIX

What Is Your Purpose?

LET'S UNPACK THIS GIFT ARCHETYPE. THERE IS A CONNECTION BETWEEN THE INTIMACY WE EXPERIENCE WITH OUR TRUE SELVES AND THE IMPACT WE HAVE ON THE LIVES OF OTHERS. We discussed earlier the power we possess when we are intimate with ourselves. The procreative power that occurs when we truly know ("*yada*"[27]) ourselves. The connecting tissue between our intimacy with our true self and the impact we have on others is our calling. Our calling is the charge we were given before we were even placed on this planet. To explain this in more detail, let me breakdown this gifting trinity. Our calling is the task or action that we are called to do. To use the Superman analogy, Superman's calling was to fight evil in Metropolis. His purpose was to protect Metropolis. His gift was being superhuman. This calling, however, did not begin in Metropolis, but in Smallville. He went from Smallville, a tiny Midwest existence, to a bustling big city existence. It occurred as a result of Clark experiencing a realization that there was something unique about himself. He possessed something that no one else possessed. It differentiated him from everyone else in his life. Clark's gift became evident within the construct of a

---

27 *yada* is a Biblical Hebrew word, יְדַע, that means to "to know" in both the biblical and literal sense.

Smallville existence. Smallville was the best place for the revelation of Clark's gift, but it was not the best place for him to operate in it.

Clark's extraordinary talent was revealed because in a place like Smallville, being different is not something that is the norm. Conformity is usually the rule of the day. But because this was who Clark truly was, his gift, superhuman strength, was all the more pronounced. Many times we lament over our small beginnings. The places where we feel misunderstood or constrained. We search for significance and prominence instead of being true to ourselves and others. It is trueness in any situation and circumstance that brings about significance in our lives, not our desire for it. Superman did not go from Smallville to the Metropolis because he desired it. His gifting trinity propelled him there. His gift revealed was the catalyst for moving him toward Metropolis.

Many times, our gift, once revealed, cannot stay in the place of revelation, like the story of Jesus who was born in a dark, filthy manger in sleepy Bethlehem. The culmination of His calling, however, occurred in Jerusalem, the seat of King David's kingdom. Illumination shines brightest in spaces where there is lack of light. Your gift does not illuminate in a space of light, but in those places where there is a void of the very thing you possess. Instead of looking at the lack of light as a problem to your vision, you be the light. When you illuminate these dark spaces, more is revealed. Your purpose is revealed. Always having been right there in front of you, but needing you to light up the space so it can be illuminated to you. We look outside ourselves for so many things, but it is who we are and what we do that reveals so much to us. The tragedy in life is that many people die waiting for a sign to act. Tragically only realizing that the sign would be revealed the moment they take action. Built into their action is the sign. Are you waiting for a sign? Beware, because the sign you seek externally is within you. It is the hero in action within you.

One of the greatest tactics to discourage and distract us from that perfect space of executing our trinity gifting is the tendency to make everything polemic. In other words, in understanding things we find distinctions in an adversarial way versus first seeing how these things can work together. There is a place for the adversarial and the polemic, but with respect to understanding, it is a liability. Let me give an example in marriage.

My wife and I are completely different. Over the last thirty years we have at times seemingly been engaged in battle. We love each other, so the question must be asked, why? People do not get married because they desire to live in conflict, so why does it seems to devolve into what seems like war at times? The answer can be found in this simple word, perspective. How we view each other and how we view marriage. You see, neither of us came from environments that fostered cohesiveness in marriage. The previous marriages we came from were both contentious, and eventually ended in divorce. This framed our perspectives. We married without having addressed this issue. Now, if no disagreement ever occurred in our marriage, there is a possibility we could have moved along without conflict. The likelihood of this, is somewhere between slim and none. The more likely response we will give to conflict will be born out of the examples that were demonstrated before us. This is why people who get divorced tend to come from divorces. Consider this statistic: You are 40%

more likely to get a divorce if your parents were divorced.[28] The bottom line is we are predisposed to replicating behaviors we've seen before, despite having witnessed them fail. To truly be in a divine space, we must both be able to fight this response and see ourselves in our fullness, our spiritual wholeness and marital oneness. We must be able to see the divine within us, the *Imago Dei*, the image of God rather than our human frailty.

The key to the marriage, for me, was not to become fixated on our differences, but rather to focus on how our differences are connected, like pieces in a jigsaw puzzle. When we see a puzzle piece, we do not hold up two pieces looking for similarities. We hold them up to find how they connect. We look for the place where one part of a puzzle piece fits  into another. This revelation helped me to understand my spouse, and how the things she did that drove me up the wall were actually intentional on the part of God. I stopped focusing on how we differed, and started seeing how we complemented one another. Nothing changed except my perspective.

Now, you don't go from revelation to transformation overnight, but we are on the right path. In the thirty year span of our relationship, I have personally gone from saying and believing we weren't going to make it, to thinking about how far can we go together. This is what you must

---

28 Source: Nicholas Wolfinger, Understanding the Divorce Cycle, Cambridge University Press, 2005

do. Do not look at your life from the prism of why this isn't the way you would like it, why it shouldn't have been this way, or this should or should not have happened. Look at your life from the perspective of a jigsaw puzzle. How does this all fit together? Many times we have been given a vision of the jigsaw puzzle that is our calling, purpose, and gift. It is that vision that should guide you as you piece together the events, situations, circumstances, opportunities, and pitfalls of life. These are the pieces of the jigsaw puzzles that comprise our lives. But without a vision of the bigger picture, it will be hard to make sense of it all. When you buy a jigsaw puzzle, you do not look at the pieces first. You look at the completed puzzle pictured on the box. That is the vision. That is actually why you buy the puzzle in the first place. To see that picture come to life. That picture guides you. If you do not know the vision, what the picture looks like, when we get a piece that seems out of place, we bemoan its existence instead of trying to see how it all fits together. When we get the right perspective, we find the bigger picture is you in your rightful place, doing what you were created to do, answering the call on your life, accomplishing your purpose and operating in your gift.

You cannot bless others until you can see the blessing within your story. Clarity of what you are doing and clarity of why you are doing it. Fitting the pieces together will enable you to do the same in the lives you are called to impact. You are here not for your own benefit, but for those you are most suited to bless. It is part of the divine order. This manifests when you can help others see themselves become whole. You recognize these people when you see them attempting to solve their puzzle of life. When you have solved the puzzle of who you are and what is your gift, you will be drawn to those attempting to solve their puzzles. When they see your finished puzzle, they will be drawn to you as well. They will see your picture and it will help them make sense of theirs.

Questions To Ask Yourself (Chapter 6):

Write down what you think is your purpose? What do you think is your calling? What does your life puzzle's picture look like?

Are you currently in a situation (job, relationship) that doesn't feel right to you?

What is your Smallville?

What is your Metropolis?

PATRICK PETE

CHAPTER SEVEN

Who Are You Called To Impact?

I REMEMBER IT LIKE IT WAS YESTERDAY. I WAS LISTENING TO TONY ROBBINS ON A MOTIVATIONAL TAPE. HE SAID SOMETHING THAT STRUCK ME LIKE A BOLT OF LIGHTNING. HE SAID, "THE SECRET TO LIVING IS GIVING."[29] Of all the things I would expect Tony Robbins to say, that wasn't it. I am sure that if I had heard this at any other stage in my life, I wouldn't have paid any attention to it. But at that moment, it was profound. I had lived a little, been married a while, raised a family, been heavily involved in church, and worked successfully within the corporate world. I knew that what he was saying was true. Regardless of what we do, until we live a life that blesses others, we will have a void in our life. We are social beings by nature. Our connectedness to each other is an integral part of our overall well-being.

In an article published by "Psychology Today" the following was stated, *"Babies not held, nuzzled and hugged enough will literally stop growing, and if the situation lasts long*

---

24 "The Secret To Living Is Giving - Tony Robbins." Accessed June 3, 2017. https://www.tonyrobbins.com/leadership-impact/the-secret-to-living-is-giving/.

enough, even if they receive proper nutrition, die."[30] When we think about what Tony Robbins stated, that the secret to living is giving, the previous statement makes complete sense. If a baby stops growing and eventually dies because they were starved of social interaction, then experiencing a hallmark of social interaction—giving —should and does make us feel all the more alive. How does this relate to our discussion? Your trinity of gifting means little if it doesn't impact those who you were created to bless with it. Just as the importance of social interaction is directly correlated to our physical well-being, likewise, it is important to note that this same principle also applies to our destiny. Your destiny is directly tied to those who are most affected by it. Not only does this provide a sense of being alive, but it is the connection that facilitates life in all of us. Your destiny, your trinity of gifting, and their intended destination, those called to be impacted, are intrinsically connected. It is the conduit of life.

Who are you called to impact? Most often they are people who can identify with you and your story, people who connect with your message. Earlier in chapter four we talked about how people seek heroes as they attempt to find their own identity. This is part of our innate need to connect as humans. An identity is sought. As social beings, we attempt to connect with those with whom we see these similarities. It is part of our tribal nature. It's the reason why we have hundreds of different nations, and within them even more ethnicities. There are 195 coun-

---

30 Szalavitz, Maia. "Touching Empathy." Psychology Today. Sussex Publishers, LLC, 01 Mar. 2010. Web. 12 Apr. 2017. <https://www.psychologyto-day.com/blog/born-love/201003/touching-empathy>.

tries[31], and so many ethnicities, that to quantify them accurately is nearly impossible. If we look at language alone, there are approximately six thousand different languages spoken in the world. My point is, your journey helps shape your story. Your story is what shapes your message. Your message is what impacts those you are called to reach.

In chapter four we go through the different stages of your journey to true heroism. It is important that you are self aware as you walk through this journey because there will be key moments along the way that you will need to identify opportunities. These key moments will be critical as you go from story to message. Let's chronicle my journey starting with the call.

In hindsight, I can now see that I always knew my calling. It shaped my youth, albeit in a distorted way. It shaped my young adult life. Even as I contemplated marriage, my calling was a driving motivation with respect to the decisions I made. Here was the problem. Because I was not self aware I did not realize this was what I was doing. As a young boy I always wanted to be in charge of things. I ended up being kind of a bully, albeit not a very good one, thank God!

What I didn't understand is that I was called to lead. So I reacted based on what I was feeling versus responding to my calling. It is the difference between the wise and the foolish. Sadly, too many

> **The path to greatness is littered with struggles, tests and trials...be wary of paths that seem easy or comfortable.**

---

31 Independent States in the World. (2018, May 30). Retrieved February 3, 2019, from https://www.state.gov/s/inr/rls/4250.htm

people lack the ability to know the difference. We discussed some of this in chapter 3. I had something pushing me but did not have the right environment or the right guidance to do anything with it. Like a child placed in the driver's seat of an amazing sports car, I nearly crashed my life instead of driving it to my destiny. The key to ensuring your life drives you to your destiny is ensuring that you have a driver who knows the car and your destiny. For me. this is not me, but God.

As I grew older, this calling tormented me because I didn't understand it. This led to an abject fear of it growing up. Despite this fear, I continued to make decisions along the lines of my calling. When I met my wife and her young son, it was my calling that drove me into marriage. I saw myself as someone who could be a blessing to them. This was born out of the lack of shepherding in my own life: the struggles I witnessed my mother experience, and the damage that I both witnessed and experienced as a result of the absence of my father operating in his gift. This left an enduring impression on me. I was compelled to avoid doing the same. I saw my wife and her son as the embodiment of my mother and I. I married not realizing my calling was driving it. I experienced it while in the military and while in leadership in my church.

My calling was driving me at every turn, but I was unaware. It was not until I came to a place of crisis that it all became clear. Who I was, why I was here, and what I was called to do. This is the crossroad. The place where confusion and clarity meet in battle. Depending upon the examples in your life and the guide you have chosen, or better yet chose you, what the outcome of the battle will be may end in triumph or tragedy. You see, what I found in my hero's journey is that choosing between chaos and clarity is not as simple a choice as we may think. There are a number of variables involved and, based upon the values that you have embraced, these variables will either equate to a right choice or a wrong one. If the examples set before you are ones that introduced confusion and chaos into your life, you may believe you will choose clarity because it appears to be a clear choice, but as was stated earlier, we often follow what we see exemplified before us versus what we deductively process. In other words, when we make decisions many of us do not make them after having thought out what to do. We simply react instinctively, on emotion. Our instincts are what we are conditioned to do. This is not a recipe for success, unless you are conditioned to do the right thing, of course. This is why having a guide, mentor, or coach is critical. I would even dare to say it is a must. As the saying goes, "Two heads are better than one." Let me use my guide, Pastor John Kenneth Jenkins Sr., and my time under his leadership, as an example to show how the right guide and environment can set you on the path to your trinity of gifting, even when you don't yet realize it.

When I arrived at First Baptist Church of Glenarden (FBCG), I was nowhere near moving into my calling, purpose and gift. Little did I know God was directing the scene to set me on the course toward my destiny: being the "The Gift Coach." Before having come to FBCG, I honestly was in a state of confusion. I wouldn't say it was chaotic, I wasn't in the storm, but I could hear the windows clamoring and the thunder cracking. Pastor Jenkins's teaching was the first time I heard principles, teachings, and values that could quiet the storm around my life. I swallowed it hook, line, and sinker. The environment allowed me to grow and the quiet allowed me to get my bearings. It also set in motion the events that would ultimately send me into my gifting. This path, however, was one that was not absent of obstacles and struggles. To say it was pleasurable would be ridiculous, but to say it was simply rewarding is also an understatement. It was beyond rewarding. It was life changing and transformative. That is the way it is on the path to greatness. It is littered with struggles, tests and trials. It is for this reason we should always be wary of paths that seem easy and comfortable. None of those qualities have any relationship with greatness. They are insidious traps to mediocrity.

Remember when I said earlier I swallowed my mentor's teaching hook, line, and sinker? There is only one problem with the hook, line, and sinker mentality; you will struggle to be mobile enough to move when God instructs you to do so. You run the risk of making your focal point the instrument of His Power in your life versus God being the Source of that Power. Fortunately for me, God made me in such a way that I am adept at spitting out hooks. What I mean is my mistake wasn't being dedicated to my mentor, his teaching, and the environment he established. That was one of the best decisions I ever made. My mistake was assigning the pressure of power to him and not to the source of power from which he was getting his strength, God. I say this to you because many people on the journey will ascribe too much power to their guide or mentor. They are there to guide you, but not to become a crutch for you. Let me use the moon and moonlight to illustrate this point.

Moonlight has been instrumental in so many human events, such as love, war, art, etc. The significance of moonlight is that it provides light in the midst of darkness. The moon, however, is not the source of the light. The sun is the source. The moon merely reflects the sunlight. The moon, put simply, is a rock in the sky. But its relationship to the sun enables it to guide sailors at sea, inspire love between two people, or artists to create, and the list can go on and on. All of this from a rock. The guide is important, but the journey is more important. Never get caught staring at the moon when you have a destiny to reach. Get back to the journey.

My life was transformed at FBCG and I felt compelled to give back to the place that had so impacted my life. One of the most important elements to the hero's journey is the desire and motivation to give back. A hero is inherently a giver. If you are a taker, you are veering toward the dark side. You are, for all intents and purposes, a villain. At the heart of taking is selfishness. Which, in and of itself, is not inherently wrong, with one exception; when that selfishness comes at the expense of others. This is true evil, which is why regardless of the motivation, stealing from someone is frowned upon on every level. It is selfishness at the cost of depriving someone else of something they earned or possessed. No endeavor, regardless of the end goal, can survive an ethos built on that premise. It will be short lived no matter what. This direction does not usually happen as a result of someone stating I want to be evil or selfish. It happens because we can find ourselves veering off course. You will need a compass on the journey to your destiny to keep you on track. A compass to ensure that you reach your true destiny and not a false facsimile of it. The false facsimile is "achievement" at the cost of others. Always ensure your compass points toward your true north, giving.

My first foray into this giving was assisting the leader of the ministry that was instrumental in the transformation I experienced at FBCG. That ministry was Brother's In Discipleship, BID for short. BID is a men's discipleship group. "This ministry uses a small-group setting to bring Christian men together for an in-depth exploration of God's Word using the MasterLife curriculum." I initially went through the program and graduated, but felt no life change in me. This was not a reflection of the ministry but more a reflection of my inauthentic participation in the ministry. I learned that doing anything without authenticity is akin to a movie set. It will look real at a glance, but upon closer inspection you will see that it is all a façade. Despite having graduated, I went back through the ministry a second time. It was during this time that the course of my life was set on course.

The second time I completed BID, the transformation was real. I felt different. But more importantly, although I didn't realize it at the time, I was beginning to see purpose for my life. I was beginning to have vision. This is what happens when we begin to operate in an authentic and genuine space. When we are willing to embrace truth. Much of what I learned, which comprises chapter one of this book, was learned during this time. My life prior to the surgical exploration of who I was that occurred during BID was a lie. A lie that I had constructed in order to survive. God helped me realize this through BID. Through authentic relationships and sound principle-based teaching, I learned that what I thought of myself was not true. It was a survival mechanism. I thought of myself more highly than I ought. This created a false narrative in the one place it cannot occur, and that is in my own mind. It is virtually impossible to find and stay on the right path without authenticity, truth and a willingness to be introspective. One of my many mentors, Eric Thomas, calls the latter self assessment.

It was this self assessment that caused me to go through BID twice. I eventually became the director of BID. That is a story unto itself. As director, I watched many men go through BID. I wondered if they were any different. Had they simply completed the training but had no transformation? I called this a form of discipleship bulimia, having consumed the material only to throw it up later. Many people think achievement is the barometer for success. I don't think so. I believe transformation that results in growth is the true parameter for success. Just as the bulimic over consumes but looks emaciated, so are those who believe that achievement absent of transformation is success. They have the degrees, awards and are lauded, but they are emaciated mentally, emotionally, and spiritually. Had I not gone through BID again, I would have at a minimum greatly lengthened the time it would take me to reach my destiny. And at worst, I may not have reached it at all. However, I knew something was wrong because, despite the BID certificate, I was still starving, weak, mentally and spritually fatigued. I was not whole and I knew that BID had the right nutrition for me. But my lack of consumption left me malnourished, both as an individual and in all the roles of my life. This was the first experience that gave me insight into who I was called to impact. My own pain in my journey helped me identify those I was called to impact. When you can identify your pain within others, this is how you know who you are called to impact. Your compass will guide you, no it will compel you to help. For it is in our own pain that we connect with those who suffer likewise.

It is our triumph over that pain, however, that empowers us to help them.

Questions To Ask Yourself (Chapter 7):

(1) Can you define your pain? If so, have you overcome it?

(2) If you have overcome your pain, how did you do so? If not, what are you plans to address it?

(3) Who do you believe you are called to impact?

1. Yes, but no I have not overcome it.

2. My plan will be to find a mentor/counselor whom I feel comfortable & trust so that I have the boldness and security to be truthful to share this pain.

PATRICK PETE

CHAPTER EIGHT

The Needs of Those You Are Called to Impact

PEOPLE PRIORITIZE THINGS ACCORDING TO THEIR HURT. THEY WILL ADDRESS THEIR PAIN BE-FORE THEY WILL ADDRESS THEIR PLEASURE. A good correlation could be that pain and need are in many ways synonymous. It is primeval. As babies, life is not initiated through pleasure, it is initiated through pain. When babies take their first breath they cry, and when they feel hunger they cry. Crying is one of the ways we know the needs of babies, even though they cannot tell us using words. Understanding who we impact is intrinsically related to this human connection. Crying signals a need. Relationships help us connect with those we are called to impact when they cry. Whether it is the baby's cry or a person who you simply say hello to, then end up talking to for an hour about their situation. Crying is what sets off the bat signal of our gifting. The hero within us is sensitized to the needs of those we are called to impact. We need only to look within ourselves to find the void that has been filled. That area of need to help point us toward those we not only are called to impact but are uniquely gifted to be a transformative instrument of God in their lives.

This is what occurred for me in BID. I learned through relationship. Every nook and cranny of my being was involved in what I call the triad of relationship: your mentors, your peers, and your mentees. Do not miss the fact that all of the aforementioned are plural. Often there are a number of people who fill these roles. Sometimes simultaneously, but often they come and go at different periods in both your life and theirs. You must be keen to this as you interact with them. Not knowing when and when not to engage in relationships can prevent you from connecting to the right person at the right time. In each of these relationships you will find a place of either support or pain. Use of the former and solving the latter will give you a holistic approach in addressing the needs of those you are called to impact.

Let me illustrate the relationships that define my understanding of meeting the needs of those I am called to impact. Let me first say that the relationships identified below are illustrated in a metaphorical sense. While they are expressed singularly, they are a synthesis of all the people in my life who have been mentors, peers, and mentees. All of which have played an instrumental role in my life as a whole, but particularly with respect to understanding the needs of those I have been called to impact. These three relational perspectives will give you a complete vantage point of the core relationships we all engage in with respect to our calling, purpose, and gift.

Your Mentors

We talked about the guide earlier in chapter four. Your mentor may or may not be this person. Do not have expectations of finding all those who will help you on your hero's journey in one person. Remember as I mentioned earlier, the journey supersedes those who come alongside you. Never let anything or anyone dissuade you from continuing and completing your journey. The main focus of the mentor is to understand what it is you can learn that will, as we discussed earlier, allow you to be transformed throughout the journey.

I mentioned BID. My mentor was instrumental in helping me to develop and grow into the man that I would need to be in order to help those who I was called to impact. My gift was in me, but the packaging was terrible. While this does not impact the effectiveness of the gift, it does impact the ability of those I am called to impact and how they receive it. This is akin to giving someone a gift in a bag with filth and excrement on it. Even the most determined individual will think twice about attempting to retrieve the gift that is within you in this type of packaging. This is why it is paramount that we continuously work on ourselves. It is in this state that your mentors do their best work. My time with these men helped me develop into someone who could not only see myself in a true light, but through relationship I was able to see the dynamic of how to meet the needs of others, to address their pain points as it were. I am simply doing for others what was done for me, but in a way that is uniquely me according to the gift that is within me.

One of the best things about my mentors is their ability to be brutally honest. Depending upon where you are, this may be vitally important. For me, this was absolutely necessary. What I didn't need were people who wanted to sugarcoat my problems or issues. I needed surgery and they provided it. Every person was honest with me. This helped me to develop and grow. It also gave me insight into when and how this type of help is to be applied. Brutal honesty is not for everyone, but to those for whom it is required, it is an absolute necessity. Remember chapter one and the importance of embracing truth. Honesty is essential, but few can handle it when it is given in a straightforward manner. Kind of like liquor. Some people like it straight but most prefer cocktails. Regardless, you will have to drink from the cup of truth if you want to truly reach your destiny.

My mentors gave me help and guidance at various stages and different facets of my life. They helped me, with their wisdom, to make the right choices. If we are meant to help those we are called to make the right decisions, what better way than to have been in the same position as those we are called to help? In doing so we learn from those called to help us, what to do and what not to do. It is where one's need meets the person who can meet the need. It is our peers, however, who are instrumental in the execution of those choices. They are the ones that hold us accountable. A person can be given the right information, but if it is not applied then it is all for naught. Dr. Eric Thomas often states a powerful quote, "Information changes situations." My BU brother, Quest Queen expanded upon this quote by rightly adding, "Information applied changes situations." It is our peers who stand as sentinels at the gate of our execution, ensuring that our application is rightly applied.

Your Peers

So how does accountability play a role in helping us understand the needs of those who we are called to impact? Accountability with our peers helps us to ensure the information we give is impactful. I have learned that whatever our gift is, there is importance in understanding how we can ensure the needs of those we are called to impact are met. Accountability is a key factor in raising the level of certainty to a level of success. You need to have someone you give license to hold you accountable to the degree that you will submit to their counsel, even if you disagree. Accountability partners are different in that they remind you of the promises you made, both to yourself and to them. Depending upon where you are in your journey, this will determine whether you can simply be reminded of what it is you are to do or whether you need to be grabbed around the collar. In many ways this will determine who and how you will impact the needs of those you are called to impact.

Accountability is a twofold process. It helps you in execution but it also teaches you about giving. Let me take a moment to identify something again that was discussed earlier. That is the importance of humility. In chapter one, we talked about humility with respect to embracing truth. The yin and the yang of loving oneself requires humility. Humility is the key to providing the right balance to loving oneself in such a way that you are able to do so without the extreme of narcissism. There is no place where this is more important than with respect to accountability. It takes humility to be accountable to someone. It takes even more humility when someone is accountable to you, because if you are not careful you can become a hindrance. Let me give an example of what I am talking about.

In many personal development circles I have been involved with, I have noticed that accountability is a big deal. One of the phenomena I have experienced is what I call accountability arrogance. These are people who consider themselves hard charging, "get it done" types of people. They feel emboldened to challenge people about themselves and what they are doing, because they are doing things at such a high level. The problem with this is that most people are not receptive to it, so the accountability is less impactful and, in my humble estimation, less about the person being helped and more about the person who is checking people feeling good about themselves. It is usually ineffective. Now if someone gives you license to do this, and they are comfortable with it, more power to them. But what I have learned is that most people are not responsive to that type of accountability unless the person holding them accountable has an enormous love account with them. This is the reason why many mothers are effective with challenging their children. They usually are the source of love and nurturing for that person.

Let's use someone who was an accountability coach to me, Shelly Shelton. Shelly possesses a unique skillset. What makes her unique is not only her ability to be determined in holding you accountable, but also her ability to instantly connect with you in a way that allows you to know she is focused on your best interest. Usually this type of rapport has to be built up over time. But somehow Shelly can convey to you her care and concern, all the while being tough on you with respect to your goals and objectives. I probably wouldn't have completed this book without her.

This is a gift. But that isn't the point of mentioning her. The point is that having come into contact with her allowed me to experience a unique gifting that empowers me when I am engaged with those whose need I am designed to meet. It shows me through relationship how to be the most effective when engaged with those I am called to impact. Because my relationship with Shelly gave me the vantage point of those whose needs I am impacting, my mentees.

Your Mentees

Of these three relationships, the most important in understanding the needs of those you are called to impact is that of the mentee. How can you truly meet the needs of anyone unless you know them? Well I suppose you can impact anyone incidentally, but if there is a true intention to impact, then knowing them is essential. In fact, it goes to the heart of what it means to meet those needs. When you impact without truly knowing them it becomes transactional rather than transformational. Let's focus on the importance of a transformational relationship versus a transactional relationship.

When I say a relationship is transformational, I mean that it is based on the who and not the what. The individuals involved are the focal point as opposed to a particular task. The objective is the well-being of the individuals involved in the relationship. Let's use the relationship of parent and child. The focal point in this relationship is the growth and the development of the relationship itself, not the roles or responsibilities involved. Its existence should result in the betterment of those involved in the relationship. The roles and tasks within the relationship are the result of this paradigm. Each individual's concern is primarily focused on those they are in relationship with versus a transactional relationship.

Transactional relationships exist for the purpose of the execution of a task. One cannot ascertain need from transactional relationships. Needs are rarely met in these circumstances because those who execute the tasks, absent of some level of relational connection, cannot truly know whether the need is met, only that the task has been completed. Let's use the mother/child analogy. A mother who simply hears a baby cry can execute the task of feeding them, but without relational connection cannot truly know whether the baby's needs are met. The baby may continue to cry even when the task of feeding is completed. It is the connection between a mother and baby that lets the mother know exactly what to do in order to meet the baby's needs. Again, we see the connection between the transformational and the divine, the God space. Babies don't always stop crying because the task is met. They stop crying because their need is met. They are not only hungry for food, but they are hungry for the presence of their mother.

It is relationship that binds the satisfier of the need with the person in need. We connect to those we are called to impact through the relationships we develop during our journey. These relationships help us learn the different facets of having needs and meeting needs. As you experience life along your hero's journey, be sure to take notes along the way. It is important for you to do so because it gives you clarity about where you are on the journey and which direction you need to go next.

Ensure that you take a moment, if you have not already done so, to reflect on your journey. What relationships have you developed? What lessons have you learned? Where do you see yourself at this present moment? Where do you see yourself headed? All of these questions are good things to meditate on and contemplate because as you move forward on the journey, it is important to get your bearings.

Mentees

Peers

Questions to Ask Yourself (Chapter 8):

What relationships have you developed?

Gift of Serving, Giving

What lessons have you learned?

Great Listener

That I have ~~to be able to let~~ have to be careful that I don't allow the ppl I mentor become dependant on met

What direction do you see yourself headed??

know when to let them ~~grow~~ grow and rely on God and not me.

I want to continue to grow in my gift of mentoring ~~and~~ my struggle is that I am an introvert, but once I get to know ppl I ~~can~~ will poor into them

CHAPTER NINE

Where Are You?

In chapter three we discussed the YOU spectrum. We talked about how on one end lies the perverted or distorted you, and on the other end lies the true you. For the sake of clarity, we will use the word perverted to describe both the perverted and distorted, but in explanation we will articulate how these two have nuanced differences. The perverted you, as described in chapter three, is the extreme. It is the complete opposite of who you were created to be. The path to that extreme is a path of distortion. We are rarely distorted in the womb. It is when we move in the wrong direction that we experience distortion. If we continue on this path, we become a full distortion, which inevitably devolves into fullon perversion. We become something that not only negatively impacts us, but negatively impacts the world. The other extreme is the true you. This is our ultimate objective. The place where we epitomize who we were created to be. This is the path of growth and transformation. The embodiment of knowing, mastering, and operating in our gift. The place we find our own fulfillment as well as add value to the world.

The other extreme is the true you. This is our ultimate objective. The place where we epitomize who we were created to be. This is the path of growth and transformation.

The embodiment of knowing, mastering, and operating in our gift. The place we find our own fulfillment as well as add value to the world.

The other ingredient is your place on the hero's journey. The hero's journey is expressed in detail in chapter four, we will not go into it here other than to say that where we are on that journey is important to answering the question asked in the title of this chapter.

If the YOU spectrum lets you know where you are in terms of your own development as an individual, the hero's journey lets you know where you are with respect to the direction of your path to your destiny. The nexus of these two things, your position on the YOU spectrum and your position on the hero's journey, could be described as the longitude and latitude of where you are at in life. They are your life coordinates.

Knowing your life coordinates is of supreme importance with respect to how successful you will be in knowing, mastering and operating in your gift. A person who knows themselves and is engaged in the hero's journey has a life coordinate that places them in the right positioning for a successful, fulfilled life. Conversely, those of us who are in places of advanced distortion or perversion, and are not engaged in the hero's journey, are in positions of unhealthiness and unfitness for success and fulfillment. "YOU spectrum" fitness relates to our fitness as individuals with respect to our hero's journey. As you read earlier, without this fitness, the journey has a high probability of failure.

Here is the beauty of the interdependence of the YOU spectrum and the hero's journey. Deficiencies in either can be addressed by strengths in the other. The hero's journey itself can be transformative, in and of itself. The closer you are to the true you the more likely you are to find yourself embarking on the journey and the more likely you are to be successful. Let me give you a personal example.

When I began my journey, I didn't even realize I was on a journey. My trajectory was initially a byproduct of my upbringing. Truth is big in my family and lying is probably the most despised thing you can do. While I was neither close to my true self early in my life or on an intentional journey to discover my gifting, I did have ingrained in me a hatred for lying and a love for truth. This helped me once I began a genuine pursuit for purpose. I began to explore everything with the hope that it would enable me to accomplish my purpose in life. I studied other religions. I even explored different forms of Christian community from the familiar Christian communities of my upbringing, the Catholic and Baptist church, to nondenominational, to home churches. I went to seminary and I read various religious texts. What I discovered was a deficiency within myself. I realized, in hindsight, that this was my hero's journey. My pursuit of a better me led me to taking the hero's journey

Through self examination I could identify areas of concern within myself. In chapter one, we talked about why the ability to embrace truth is important. This is a perfect example. If you are not able to embrace truth, you will not be able to identify these deficiencies. I would not have been able to recognize these issues and I would not have grown as a person. I have mentioned it a number of times in this book, but it is worth repeating with one addition. Truth, pain, growth, and life are inextricably connected.

The aforementioned are essential to living a true and authentic life. What connects them is pain. Truth is often painful. Growth involves pain. Birth of life involves pain. The essence of physical death is when the cells can no longer replicate. They cease to grow and then they die. Lack of growth signifies death. It only stands to reason then that the presence of growth itself signifies life. There are numerous examples of this, birth being one of them. I want to focus on one component in particular. The one component that I hope I have consistently conveyed as crucial.

All of these components are interconnected and important, but truth is the catalyst. Truth is what must be present in order for everything else to work. I am reminded of what scientists do when they look for life on other planets. They look for the catalyst: water. If they see water, they have hope that life is possible. Truth is to your calling, purpose and gift, what water is to life.

Now before we go too far into developing this concept, I want to bring us back to the point of the discussion, and that is the interdependence of the YOU spectrum and the hero's journey. The interdependence of the two is vital, but depending upon where you are in either process, that interdependence may not be strong. Truth is what fortifies the interdependence. If truth is present you will have the ability to strengthen that interdependence. This, in turn, will enable you to bridge any gap. You can pinpoint your location and begin the process of moving in the direction of your triumph. Once you know your coordinates, you can map and track the movement toward your destiny. Your destiny is the point where the true you and your gifting trinity meet. This is where you are trying to reach. Knowing your coordinates will allow you to have the feeling of a person on a mission who has a map. The key to winning in war and in life is knowing your position on the battlefield and ensuring you hold the best strategic position. Even if you cannot see the target, knowing your position and knowing the coordinates of your destiny will allow you to get within range of it. Once you do this, effort will carry you the rest of the way.

These two components, the YOU spectrum and the hero's journey, comprise the latitude and longitude of your position on the board of the game of life, the current coordinates in our lives. When you are at the life coordinates of the true you who has discovered the hero within, you have arrived at the location of your destiny. Now it's time to get started. A hero's work does not begin when they realize they are heroes. It begins when they begin to act heroically.

Questions To Ask Yourself (Chapter 9):

Do you feel you know where you are at? If so, write down in your own words where is that place?

Are you prepared to make the changes necessary if where you are at isn't where you want to be?

Express your life coordinates by identifying 1-10 where you are on the YOU Spectrum, 1 being a perverted you and 10 being the true you.

PATRICK PETE

The Metamorphosis

BUTTERFLIES ARE MEANT TO FLY

CHAPTER TEN

Start: Unleashing the Hero Within

ALL OF THE PREVIOUS CHAPTERS SERVED ONE PURPOSE, TO GET YOU TO THE PLACE OF START- ING. KNOWING WHERE YOU ARE, HAVING A MAP, AND KNOWING YOUR DESTINATION ARE ALL OF LITTLE IMPORTANCE IF YOU HAVE NO INTENTION OF TRAVELING. Everything is about moving, acting, be- ginning. One of my coaching clients, Janice Leono Moss, made a powerful statement on one of my podcasts, "The Your Gift Conference". She gave a testimony of speaking in a Facebook group that is a part of our online community, Breathe University. She said, "Some things cannot be acti- vated until we act!" I know so many people who struggle with starting. They pontificate about how they can't do this or that until they have this or that. I realize there is some truth to this, but the problem is that many people are in a perpetual state of preparation. Listen, I don't want to, in any way, lessen the importance of preparation, but there are some things that cannot be known or prepared for until we act. There are many over-the-counter ointments and salves that have a number of things in the ingredients, but they always have a section that says "active ingredient".

When we are at the place of unleashing the hero within, the active ingredient is action.

What then is the impediment to acting? I have found that it is one's belief in themselves. Most people are immobilized from acting because of a lack of belief in themselves. My hope and intention is that this is the least of your issues if you have read through this book. At the end of the day, that is the entire point of the book. If you know where you are, you should either be in a place of knowing yourself or in the process of knowing yourself. If you have read through this book you realize that you should not only know yourself, but in doing so have an intimacy with yourself such that you are comfortable with both your strengths and weaknesses. You should love yourself. If you have read through this book you should be on a quest to knowing your calling, your purpose, and your gift. It is in the quest of your hero's journey that you manifest the hero in action.

Every hero has a journey. The journey itself is simply the process by which a person gains clarity. The existential question, *"Why am I here?"* is answered. The real work and impact is what we do with the hero within us. Do we unleash them or do we simply revel in the knowledge without effect? Heaven forbid if we embrace the latter. The purpose of the hero is not to stand with their hands on their hips and their chest stuck out, posing. The purpose of the hero is to be a beacon. A beacon in the sense of being a lighthouse of hope for those whose needs you are meant to meet. Earlier in chapter eight, we talked about identifying the needs of those we are called to impact. We made a correlation between our gift and the needs of those we are called to impact. The inverse of that is that those who are in need are seeking something to fill the void. The baby's cry or the bat signal are all signals of need. Signals to the hero within us all, that when sent out, beckons to our hero's ear. They compel us to respond! Before we go further I need to be clear about some-thing. Whether or not you come to a place in your life where you embrace your triple gifting, I think it is important we understand that to not do so has grave implications.

I follow a powerful motivational and inspirational speaker, Eric Thomas. He is one of the top motivational speakers in the world, right up there with Tony Robbins, Les Brown, Willie Jolley and others. One of the things I noticed was that many of the people who follow him have on occasion said, "Thank you, ET! had it not been for you and what you are doing, I wouldn't be here! I was going to take my life but I attended one of your conferences or I heard you or saw you on YouTube and I didn't do it!" As I listened to these testimonies something occurred to me. What if ET had not accepted his calling, understood his purpose, and walked in his gift? What might have been the outcome for hundreds of thousands of people?

There is no way to be definitive about the outcome, because I am not a prophet, but I do not believe it's much of a stretch to say it is highly likely they may not be here had ET not embraced who he was and do what he is doing. Write this down, *"If you can save lives by operating in your gift, you can easily put lives at risk by not operating in your gift."* In the case of those who walk in the opposite direction and become a perverted version of themselves, the outcome can be catastrophic. Let us think seriously and soberly about this. The hero is not built for the lounge chair. They are built for the air. A hero not being heroic breaks the very fabric of the universe. It is a serious responsibility. We even said as much in the hero's journey when we speak of the "Fear of the Call". As the biblical verse states, *"From everyone to who has been given much, much more will be demanded; and from the one who has been entrusted with much, much will be asked."*[26] This everyone means everyone. You have been entrusted with a beautiful, wonderful gift. You may not realize what is your gift, but rest assured, you have one. You have been given custody of that gift for a reason. To not honor it would be criminal. Let me share a biblical parable to bring home this point. The parable of the talents.

In the Bible, there is a parable within the Gospels where Jesus tells the story of a master who had three servants.[27] Each servant had a certain number of talents that the master had entrusted to them while he traveled. The first servant was given five talents, the second two talents, and the third one talent. Upon his return, each servant went to the master to show him what they had done with the talents he gave them. The first servant doubled the talents given to him. He returned ten talents for five. The second servant returned four for two. The third servant, however, had buried the one talent he was given and simply returned it back to the master with all manner of excuses for why he had done so.

What needs to be understood is the response the master had for each servant. The first two he commended and used a familiar phrase that many Christians know very well, *"Well done, good and faithful servant, you have been faithful over a few things, now I will make you ruler over many*

---

26 Luke 12:48 - New International Version (NIV)

things, enter into the joy of the Lord."[28] To the last, however, he also uses familiar phraseology that we hear with respect to one particular response from the master, damnation. He says, "You wicked and lazy slave . . . As for this worthless slave, throw him into outer darkness, where there will be weeping and gnashing of teeth." This last statement just happens to be the same language, in many religious circles, used to describe someone who is going to hell. I am not here to argue any religious theological views, but I mention that parable because there is a universal truth there. That truth is that when we are given something of value meant to bless others, it is not optional to do something with it. When you possess a gift, you have a responsibility to know it, master it and operate in it. There are people who depend on you to do so. Whether you believe it or not there is a transcendent responsibility attached to it. But there are levels to this we must prepare, plan, and execute.

As an IT professional, I have learned this principle in many different variations. I learned it from a biblical perspective. I learned it as a sailor in the Navy. I learned it in my professional career. What is it? It is the importance of preparation. We have discussed so much leading up to this point. One would think we could simply act. I have learned that even when it is seemingly apparent, we can never foresee all that could happen. It is incumbent upon us to prepare ourselves. The hero in action is no different. So, what does preparation mean? What does it look like?

Preparation is the time we spend moving into the procreative space. Pregnancy is preparation for life. There is a faithful saying, *"Suppose one of you wants to build a tower.*

---

28 Matthew 25:23 - King James 2000 Bible

Won't you first sit down and estimate the cost to see if you have enough money to complete it?"[29] You must sit down and process what it is you are preparing to do. This is preparation to execute, not to ponder whether to execute. Like the runner preparing for the race. The runner understands their race. They become familiar with the requirements for the race. They condition themselves for the race. But most importantly, they strategize how they will run the race in order to win. Strategy is about a process. If we stay with the hero theme, we could say that one's gift is synonymous with the hero's superpower. You have walked the journey and triumphed to realize who you are truly. You look into the mirror and you see the superhero inside of you. The revelation of the hero and the life of the hero are two different things. This book walked us through the complex journey to discovering the hero within. But it is the life of the hero where impact occurs. The transition from revelation to reward. The process we will follow to manifest one's gift.

Superpower or whatever you would like to call it, is comprised of two key areas of preparation: personal development and entrepreneurship. Knowing your gift, mastering your gift, and operating in your gift are what personal development within the gift philosophy is comprised of. The other part, entrepreneurship, is comprised of product development, audience engagement, and sales and marketing.

I want to begin this paragraph with a quote that I think does an excellent job of articulating what we are about to discuss. It is a quote from the great Larry Bird. It states, *"A winner is someone who recognizes his God-given talents,*

29

works his tail off to develop them into skills, and uses these skills to accomplish his goals."[30] I wanted to quote this statement because I want you to see the correlation between being a winner, operating in your gift and the hero in action. A winner is someone who recognizes his God-given talents. He knows his gift. He works his tail off to develop them into a skill, mastering his gift. He uses these skills to accomplish his goals. He operates in his gift. They are virtually identical, which seems amazing, but in actuality it makes complete sense. The principles of success, of winning, and of operating in your gift all are governed by the same universal principles: knowing, mastering, and operating.

There is one exception with respect to the Larry Bird quote and the philosophy of your gift making room for you. Operating in your gift is focused on others, whereas Mr. Bird's focus is on one's own goals. This is important because as we talk about reward I want us to remember earlier in the book when we stated that giving is what makes us feel alive. This is our reward when we realize that our existence has manifested itself in bettering the lives of others. Let me break this statement down and show how it anchors the whole gift philosophy that undergirds this book.

There are two key aspects to a statement derived from a biblical text[31], *"Your Gift will make room for you"*. There is the "Your Gift" portion, and then there is the "will make room for you" portion. I mentioned this earlier in the chapter, but I want to expound upon it here. At the heart of the gift philosophy is the burning passion and desire to witness

---

30 "Larry Bird Quotes." Accessed June 26, 2017. http://www.notable-quotes.com/b/bird_larry.html.

31 Proverbs 18:16 New King James Version (NKJV)

everyone discover with crystal clear clarity who they are, what they are called to do, and the beautiful unique gift they have been given in order to be a blessing to the world.

At this stage in the process you will have discovered who you are and your gift. This is one of the many results of the hero's journey. Now we do as Mr. Bird so eloquently stated, "work our tails off". We focus on the mastery of our gift. We go to work. So, what does mastery of our gift look like? It looks like consistency in practice and perseverance in effort.

You need to ensure that each day you are doing something to move yourself closer to perfecting your gift. Working to move from simply doing to being. There is a widely accepted theory that it takes ten thousand hours of practice to master a skill. As is the case with any theory, there are those who dispute the theory's assertion. There are many factors, such as mindset, that are important to mastery. But make no mistake about it, practicing for hours plays an important part. For the purpose of this process, I want to ascribe to this theory realizing that other factors are important, mindset being one of them. But I think it is critical to stress that consistent and persistent action play a role in mastery. Our focus for mastery is to meet the needs of others. True mastery is only complete once we have taken that mastery and began operating in our gift. Operation in one's gift is the final step in mastery. Just as practice is only truly impactful when what we do is used in the game, operating in your gift is analogous to the game.

If this were the only requirement, we could complete the circle. But this is only half of the equation, for operating in one's gift without the room to do so is the equivalent of calling a closet a home. A closet may be a domicile, but there isn't much living you can do in one. Consider these examples: Michael Jordan is magical on the basketball court and Michael Jackson comes alive on stage. The impact of your gift is lessened without the room to wield it freely. Can you imagine either of these famous Michaels working at McDonalds? Its sounds outrageous because we have seen them operating in their gift in the environments that revealed them, but the truth is we wouldn't bat an eye if we saw them in McDonalds having never seen them swimming in the ocean of their gifting. Everyone who appears to be average are not so. They appear average because they have yet to marry their gift with the place meant to reveal it. The purpose of the entrepreneurial aspect of the process is that it gives us freedom to be effective.

There are three core components to entrepreneurship: product development, audience engagement, and sales and marketing. Let's discuss each component and their roles in your gift making room for you.

Product development is the creation of ideas revolving around ways to get your gift to those it was intended to impact. We talked about the procreative process. This is where it shines brightest. Our gift is the seed of our ideas and the products derived thereof are the branches and the fruit. Let me give my own example. My calling is developing people and motivating them to believe in themselves to the point of transformative action. It is pastoral in nature. My calling and gift have spawned life coaching and writing. Each of these branches, in turn, will produce other fruit, such as online training, books, blogs, plays and even song writing. Product development is about the process of taking the seeds of creativity, planting them, nurturing them, and harvesting them. The importance of ensuring that your gift is the seed of your product development is that your gift is uniquely tailored to meet the needs of a specific group of people, your audience.

If your gift is the seed, then product development is the farming of that seed in order to bear fruit. When you operate in your gift it creates ideas and opportunities for your gift to flourish. No one plants a seed and does not expect it to grow. We expect it to grow. We expect it to rise. We expect it to bear fruit. Our gift is no different. This book is the fruit of my gift. So how does this happen?

It happens through a willful, intentional process of idea creation. It happens by thinking about how you can deliver your gift to those it was intended to bless. Idea creation is one of the beauties of the human spirit. We find so many ways to take something and manifest various other products and benefits from it. Let's use something as innocuous as wheat. From wheat we have bread, beer, and pasta, and those are only a few of the different ways wheat is used. Think about a tree. From that we have tables, chairs, and modes of transportation, such as ships. People took the idea of crafting boats from trees and spread throughout the world via wooden boats! There are so many more examples that to name them all would require a book the size of Texas. The point is product development is about you sitting down and really thinking about the different ways your gift can be delivered to those it is intended.

The connection between knowing your gift and understanding those you are called to impact is essential. Clarity and understanding of that connection is at the heart of your gift making room for you. Your gift is crafted and wrought in the fires of creation, for the express purpose of it being used to benefit your audience. Just as Excalibur is intertwined with the identity of the English, so is your gift with those who were created to benefit from it. Audience engagement is about seeking and making that connection. Everything you need to know about your audience is outlined in chapters seven and eight of this book. We talked about your gift, who it is created to impact, and whose needs it is meant to meet.

Audience engagement is the alchemy of the aforementioned. It is here we engage that audience from a business perspective. So, let's revisit product development and audience engagement. If these two are solidly established, then the last part, sales and marketing, will be built from it. Sales and marketing are about persuasion and influence. It is about identifying a need, and then convincing your audience that you can meet that need. When you develop your products with an intimate understanding of the audience that you are called to impact, the solution your audience needs will be the primary attracting force to your product. Not any slick sales or marketing techniques.

I hope you see the interdependence between your trinity gifting and the key components with respect to the entrepreneurial aspect of the gift philosophy. Your products are derived from you and your gift. Your audience is made up of those whose needs your gift meets. This is why it is absolutely a requirement to read this book and get a foundation to your pursuit of success in life. Too often we engage in an endeavor and reach the end goal, only to realize it was not what you expected or intended. When you pursue success from a firm foundation, you reach your true objective. You reach wholeness and completeness in the process. This is the process of the butterfly.

We have gone through our lives many times consuming, only to be stepped on. Our destiny, however, is not that. It is to become butterflies. Butterflies bring beauty to the world. Butterlfies help pollinate flowers that help the reproductive process of those plants. They are instructments of the fabric of life in nature. Butterflies are meant to fly. You may have slugged through your life on the ground, and into the trees of life, but that is not the intention of God. There is a butterfly inside of you. That butterfly is the gift in you. Everything in the life of a caterpillar is meant to prepare it to become a butterfly and take its first flight. The room in the life of those who know, master, and operate in their gift is the sky. The sky is the limit. .Now let's get to work.

Questions To Ask Yourself (Chapter 10):

Are you ready to get started? If so, in your own words state how you plan to do so?

What ideas have you thought about but haven't executed?

PATRICK PETE

Acknowledgements

It would be virtually impossible to acknowledge all of the people who played a part in the writing of this book. I will do my best not to forget anyone. If I have, please forgive me in advance. I want to acknowledge people in accordance with the roles they played in providing me the information, experiences, input, assistance, editing and advice.

My Mentors:

My Lord and Savior Jesus Christ, my grandfather, the Rev. E.L. Stubblefield, my grandmother, Erma Mae Hicks Stubblefield, my beloved mother, Elma Jean Sims, my father, Wilbert John Pete, my cousins Johnnie and Velma Pete, my pastor, Pastor John K. Jenkins Sr., Elder Frank Grier, Rev. Dr. Johnny Parker, Minister Elliot Moore, Deacon James Davis, Elder Stanley Featherstone, Dr. Willie Jolley, Dr. Eric Thomas, Dr. Dennis Edwards, Prof. Dick Kantzer, Dr. Doug Fombelle, Bobby Christian. I thank you all for guiding and leading me in some way or another, pointing me in the direction of my calling, purpose and Gift. Thank you.

My Peers:

To my brothers and sisters Kevin Holmes, Michael Holbrook, Milton Holt Sr., Alan Andrews, Jonathan and Miranda Williams, Donald and Rhonda Tuck, Eric Toppin Sr., Dr. Valerie Holmes, Kaimani Richards, Steve Reeves, Jamey and Tiffany Rider, Derek Bell, Terrell Randall, Yvette Judge, Annette Smith, Wendy Hicks, Tyrone and Dr. Cherylann Charles-Williamson, Shelly Shelton, Brandon and Sam Middleton, Professor Merril Holloway, Shannon Austin, Quest Green, Vickie Olatundun, Brian Keith

Thomas, Brian Thomas, Corshawn Brayboy, Marshall Fox, Dewane Mutanga, Robert "YB" Youngblood, Michael "Pops" and Rochelle T. Parks, Pierre Evans, Dr. Andriel Brice, Victor McGlothin.

My Mentees:

My beautiful daughter, Bianca Nicole Evelyn Pete. To all the men of BID whose life I may have impacted. To the many people I have mentored over the last 30 years in Information Technology. To those I led in the military. To some special people who allowed me to speak into their lives from a gift coaching perspective. To Scott Hires, Elizabeth Ellsworth, to Shane Rainey for being one of the first to believe in me and my gift. To Janice Leano Moss, Detris Pickeral, Elwyn Rainier II, Raven Hodge, Zadek Beard, Michelle Hawkins, Eric Jones Jr., Dr. Carolyn Medlock, Drea Harvey and the many others. Thank you all for the opportunity. I pray I was helpful in moving you toward your Gift. I thank and acknowledge everyone for allowing me the privilege of playing some part in your growth and God's plan for your life. Believe me I've learned as much from you all as you all have learned from me.

My Editors:

I would like to thank all of the people who helped me with the editing of this book. Charita Matthews, April Schrank, The Ellises (Linton and Dr. Jennifer Ellis) and most importantly, Eanna Roberts. Eanna, the editing process with you helped me in the one thing that was more important than simply editing my book. It made me a better writer. You may not have realized it because you were just doing your job, but I am eternally grateful for how you did it.

My Communities:

To my family (The Stubblefields, The Petes, The Hicks, The Levys, the descendents of Flossie Beasley Stubblefield Johnson, the descendents of Zulme Gabriel, The Fellowship, First Baptist Church of Glenarden, my shipmates from the Navy, my IT family, A Place Of Change Ministries (APOC), the Prayer Warriors Men's Prayerline, the Greensboro Crew, Oak Cliff in Dallas, Third Ward in Houston, the DC/Maryland/Virginia (DMV) area and last but not least my Breathe University family. Most if not all of my experiences outlined in this book were shaped in these communities.

Rest In Heaven
Chris Daniel

Chris was one of the first persons I talked to about writing a book. He was someone who counseled me, encoouraged me and supported me. We even talked about a joint book launch before God had other plans and called His son Home.

You were the epitome of someone who was a gift and knew it. You knew your gift, you mastered it and you most definitely operated in it. The world is a better place because it. Until we meet again, what a time, what a time it will be.

APPENDIX: CASE STUDIES

There is Nothing Average About You

As I prepared to complete this book, I noticed an email from a course I had taken on Coursera that recommended a book, *"The End of Average: How to Succeed in a World That Values Sameness."* by Dr. Todd Rose of Harvard University. The content of this book and the argument put forth by Dr. Todd Rose, specifically his ideas expressed in the *Science of the Individual*, so impacted me that I thought not including them in this book would be a gross dereliction of my duty as a writer. I am not only including it, but this case study is written because of it. Before I tell you why I was compelled to introduce Dr. Rose's ideas let me quickly summarize the Science of the Individual[26] as best I can.

Dr. Rose reasons that we have lived in a world that essentially evaluates individuals incorrectly. It is derived from a turn of the centaury desire to deal with the problems of a world at the advent of the industrial age. From the work of Belgian statistician, Adolphe Quetelet (pronounced "Kettle-Lay") who applied mathematical concepts to body assessment and the social issues of his day. From this along with the addition to the work of Frederick Winslow Taylor, came the concept of averagarianism which evolved into the systematic standardization of human evaluation. Taylor's scientific approach to the management of people found in his work, *"The Principles of Scientific Management"* (Frederick Winslow Taylor, 1913) set the stage for much of what many of us are very familiar with as it relates to standardization. Taylor's work is summarized in the following state-

---

26 Rose, T., & Ogas, O. (n.d.). The Science of the Individual. Retrieved November 06, 2017, from https://www.psychologytoday.com/blog/the-science-the-individual (This URL has three articles that expand on different areas where the thesis of the Science of Individual is case studied.)

ment. *"In the past, the man was first, in the future the system must be first."* This scientific approach resulted in a mindset where the system matters more than the individual in determining the individual. This is so ubiquitous within our everyday lives today that practically every aspect, from education with standardized tests, business with standardization practices within human resources, to sports with its evaluation of potential professional players, has some elements of it within all of them. For example, retail with the belief of a one size fits all mentality and stores that buy based on the standard person[27] mentality, which is why someone like myself, at 6'4", can rarely find clothes at a normal department store. So, what is averagarianism?

Averagarianism is a term that basically states that if we look at a group of individuals we can determine, based on one-dimensional factors, the ideal individual, the average man, if you will. In mathematical terms, it is akin to how we find the average of a set of numbers. The average of the numbers 1-10 is 5.5. From a Quetelain perspective this number, 5.5, represents the optimal number. While this simplistic example gives you some insight, it doesn't exactly show the real flaw in averagarianism. A better way of articulating it is expressed in Dr. Rose's book via the recounting of an issue the Air Force experienced with their pilots and their performance. Here is a brief synopsis.

The Air Force was having an enormous issue with their pilots controlling their planes. The initial finger pointed at the pilots themselves. They checked everything, the mechanics and the electronics of the plane, but they found

---

27 Ellis, K. J. (1990, July 26). Reference man and woman more fully characterized. Variations on the basis of body size, age, sex, and race. Retrieved February 13, 2019, from https://www.ncbi.nlm.nih.gov/pubmed/1704742

nothing wrong. After eliminating virtually every other possibility, they finally focused on the cockpit of the planes. In 1926, when designing the first cockpits, they gathered the measurements of hundreds of pilots. Based on these measurements, every aspects of the cockpit from size and shape of the seat to the shape of their helmets was built around the average of these measurements. They wondered if the pilots had gotten bigger. In 1950, the Air Force authorized a study of four thousand pilots and they found that none of them fit the 1926 measurements of an average man. The "average" man didn't exist. Using the averagarian paradigm, they had created a cockpit that fit no one. Instead, they began the process by which we now have adjustable seats. Steering wheels in cars that adjust up or down. They created a cockpit that adjusts to the pilot's unique dimensions. This resulted in our Air Force becoming the dominant force in the skies for generations.

Averagarianism is too expansive to go much deeper. For the sake of brevity, we will leave it at this. I would suggest, however, that you read more in depth information on this subject in Dr. Roses' book. I wanted to articulate it here because I wanted you to see where the genesis of this thought process was initiated and how it evolved into Taylorism or Scientific Management, which drives much of what we understand about standardization and how much it has impacted our everyday lives. Here are some examples that I believe you will be familiar with, and will show you how this mindset has influenced us all, and not necessarily for the better.

We determine that a person is qualified as smart based on a mean score like an IQ. If this person has a high IQ, they are smart. If this person has a low IQ, they are dumb.

It is so pervasive that it even dominates how some religious institutions deal with their congregations in the age of megachurches. The focus can move toward the congregation versus the individual members. It is a part of our vocabulary. You have heard the terms "above average" or "below average" to describe individuals. Anyone who has been in school in the past forty years has taken standardized tests. These standardized tests are so ingrained in how we deal with each other that they are used to be determinative of how a school is performing, who gets into a university, determining what is an acceptable weight. Anybody heard of the SAT or the ACT? You see it in standards for determining obesity, such as the body mass index (BMI). You see it in medical diagnosis. Let me use a very personal example.

My mother had a major heart attack. I won't go into the complexity of everything that occurred, but there was one instance that I think highlights in a very stark way the influence of averagarianism and standardization in our lives.

 After my mother had surgery to address her heart issues, it was determined that based on the data, my mother's heart was working at a left ventricular ejection fraction (LVEF) that was far lower than what was considered normal. Based on the data available to the doctor (what the book said) it was recommended my mother have an internal cardiac defibrillator (ICD) implanted into her chest. The words that were conveyed to me was the doctor said that my mother was in danger of sudden cardiac arrest. Now I am not here to de-

bate the book, nor the doctor's diagnosis. I do, however, want to make a point. The doctor didn't or couldn't account for any of my mother's uniqueness, her jaggedness. That is understandable. The doctor didn't know my mother intimately enough to factor those considerations into their diagnosis, but I did, and more importantly my mother knew herself well enough to take the doctor's recommendation and make, in my humble opinion, a more informed decision.

My mother is almost machine-like in her discipline. She has always been someone who worked out, ate right, and is obsessive about her attention to detail. The doctor couldn't account for this in their recommendations. They simply recommended what the outcome would be for the "average person" with my mother's ejection fraction numbers. I believe the doctor was incorrect. My mother didn't have the procedure.

Instead, she works out regularly, eats right, meticulously tracks her care, medications and doctor's visits. She has a

hyper-vigilant support system, our family. She is doing very well. While this example is purely anecdotal, it still compels us to question the veracity of the doctor's assertion, their dependency on the averages absent of the unique information about my mother. It will be a glorious day when we can have healthcare tailored to our jaggedness, our uniqueness as individuals, versus the average person. In business hiring practices, this mindset has dominated our approach to evaluating individuals. I have experienced interviews with people who knew nothing about my vocation, but simply made hiring decisions from predetermined assertions based on predictive assumptions about what the average candidate would or would not do.

Dr. Rose, however, proposes a different approach. I mentioned Dr. Roses' work, the Science of the Individual. The Science of the Individual is a study that focuses on the use of dynamic systems to analyze the complexity and variability of individuals with the hopes of developing a better idea of the potential of that individual. In other words, an approach determining the potential of the individual by applying systematic analysis through focus on each person's unique multidimensional variability, versus looking at them against an averagarianist approach. Dr. Rose's argument has three core principles. They are the principles of jaggedness, context, and pathways.

The jaggedness principle basically states that each individual has to possess two characteristics. They must first be multi-dimensional. Second, these dimensions must not be strongly connected. This is a simplistic explanation, but I think it is sufficient for the purpose of this book. Jaggedness and uniqueness, while not completely synonymous, do have some kinship. For the sake of this book and its purpose, let us not dismiss this relationship.

The context principle is about understanding how who we are interacts with the situations in which we act. It can be misleading if we experience how we function within a given situation, because the reality is we function differently in different situations. Who we are privately can be wholly different from who we are publicly. Context matters. Finally, there is the pathways principle.

This principle says that there are numerous pathways which are valid, but the optimal pathway is determined by our jaggedness. The myth of a pathway that is "normal" is misguided. Our pathways are self-deterministic. Again, let me reiterate, these explanations of the core principles of the Science of the Individual are rudimentary synopses. In many ways, I feel this basic articulation is almost a disservice, but this idea is so ground breaking and revolutionary that it warrants mention in this book.

Dr. Roses' work expresses, in an academic way, a similar argument to the proposition I am making in this book. Mine is different in two ways. First, I believe that Dr. Rose is speaking from a macro-perspective. He is addressing flaws in thinking that influenced the overall societal thought process. I am speaking about how the individual thinks of themselves. I have learned that many individuals are so guided by the immense influence of averagarianism and its offspring, Taylorism, that it has affected the way many people see themselves. While its impact makes it easier to systemically address certain human resource issues, the impact it has had on how people see themselves, in particular, when their jaggedness is on the edges, has had a devastatingly negative impact. Of course, the macro-influences the micro- and vice versa, but these distinctions still must be made.

Second, Dr. Rose is speaking from a scientific perspective. My argument is from the spiritual and motivational. We are all unique in our jaggedness. We must understand and know our uniqueness. We all operate differently based on differing situations, including the context. How we function within these contexts is best understood when we actively work to gain a better appreciation of how we are truly special. We all are deterministic in our pathways. In other words, the gift in you is not unlike what Dr. Rose is talking about when we integrate the three principles of jaggedness, context and pathway.

This marrying of the scientific with a spiritual context will provide you with the necessary groundwork to realize that you are a gift. My hope is that you understand we are experiencing a change. A change that is as consistent with humanity as anything. Many times the change is so enormous and massive, and happens over so long a course of time, that we miss it even while it is occurring. I hope what I have written sheds light on this paradigm shift. We are ever evolving. The need to understand ourselves and to understand the world around us is as old as human existence. The understanding of our importance in the world is one of those needs.

Winners Win, Losers Lose: Super Bowl LI

As an avid Dallas Cowboys fan, I watched Super Bowl 51 with an enormous amount of envy, but with hope. Hope because despite my team not being in the game I was rooting for the Atlanta Falcons. They looked good. Honestly, on paper they looked like a way better team than the New England Patriots, and for the most part that is exactly what it looked like in the first half of the game.

Atlanta hit New England in a way I had never seen the Patriots hit. Atlanta jumped out to a seemingly insurmountable lead (21-3) by halftime. They appeared to still be in control by the beginning of the third quarter (28-9). Then came the fourth quarter. The next series of events show, live and in color, the difference between those who win and those who lose. Winners find ways to win. Losers find ways to lose. Now before I show you this, I want to say this. I do not mean losing in a literal sense. I mean losing from a situational sense. Atlanta had an enormously successful season, but that was not their objective. Theirs, and every other team in the NFL's objective is to win the Super Bowl, so in that sense they lost, and I will tell you why. They found a way to lose. I believe it can be summed up in a series of plays in the fourth quarter. By the way, this losing mindset was not individual in nature, it was a team effort. There were extraordinarily talented players who played and made plays that were jaw dropping. Matt Ryan's QB rating for the game was 144! Julio Jones made a catch for the ages, within the series of catastrophic plays, no less. Let's dissect the series that, for me, was the series that determined the outcome of the game.

Four minutes and forty-seven seconds left in the game, Julio Jones makes an unbelievable catch to the New England 22. At this point, Atlanta is in field goal range to increase the lead by three. They run the ball for a loss, and here is where it comes off the rails. The next two plays, a sack and a holding penalty, place Atlanta out of field goal range. They were forced to punt the ball back to New England with 3:38 left, and pinned New England on their nine-yard line. Now let's set the stage for what happens next, because this really epitomizes this whole "winners win, and losers lose" concept.

With little time left, New England needs a touchdown to win, and field position-wise they were backed up. The requirements for them to win are statistically improbable. Despite all this, however, they march down the field and score the needed touchdown with a minute to spare and make a two-point conversion, itself statistically a low percentage play. Atlanta never scored again, despite having been the most prolific offense in the league that year. New England won the game. So, what was the difference? The difference is one team was in the best position to win and lost, the other team was in the worst position to win, but won.

You see the New England Patriots were so familiar with winning that even when the situation had very little opportunities for winning, the Patriots could only see those miniscule opportunities to win. They were conditioned to see them. When the opportunities to win presented themselves, they instantly recognized and seized them. Unfortunately, the Atlanta Falcons, despite having the better record and frankly having the better team at the outset of the game, weren't the better team mindset wise. They were more familiar with losing than they had been with winning, despite having been a winning team up to that point. When they experienced adversity, they were far too familiar with the feelings of losing that they instinctively responded in kind. With apologies to the Falcons, the city of Atlanta and their fans, my point is less to disparage an excellent team and more to highlight this point: winning and losing are mindsets. If you are not achieving your goals and objectives, it is likely not whether you can achieve them or not. It is likely an issue of mindset. Change your mindset, change your life.

A Still Small Voice

Oprah Winfrey is arguably one of the most famous, influential, richest people in the world. Without knowing much about her, who she is or what she does, I doubt that you would assume that she is an African American female born poor in Mississippi to a teenage mother. You would not assume that she was someone who experienced repeated sexual abuse from the place she should have received love, safety and security, her family. Despite this traumatic beginning, however, Oprah Winfrey is not only all of the aforementioned, but she has become a philanthropic tour de force. She has established schools for young girls around the world. She has given to well over thirty charities. The list goes on and on. When someone does as much as Ms. Winfrey has done, has affected as many lives and has placed such an indelible mark on the world in this manner, the question must be asked: how did she do it? To answer that question would require an entire book unto itself, but I believe Ms. Winfrey has left us a clue. What I want to do is highlight something she has stated in several interviews, on TV shows, and in commencement addresses. The spiritual element to her journey. What she calls that "still small voice".

Oprah Winfrey frequently recounts the story of watching her grandmother hang clothes while she was churning butter in poor, rural Mississippi as a four-year-old. I won't recount the entire story again, but I want to make a statement. Let's be clear, I am not here to promote my beliefs, but I am here to present an argument grounded in my Biblical faith. That argument being that our destiny, purpose, whatever you want to call it, is grounded in something transcendent of ourselves. I believes this story told by Ms. Winfrey highlights and helps to bring some clarity to the idea that the Creator is driving us and moving us in the right direction. Ms. Winfrey recounts with crystal clear clarity how despite her grandmother's proclamation to watch her as she hangs those clothes so that she would know how to do it, Ms. Winfrey knew that was not to be her future, her destiny, her fate, at four! Ms. Winfrey speaks of a still small voice that guided her to this truth about herself. To this day that still small voice guides her. Let us not gloss over this powerful story, because I believe that voice is the voice of God.

In the book of Jeremiah, God speaks to Jeremiah in what I believe is a similar fashion, the following words, *"Before I formed you in the womb I knew you, and before you were born I set you apart; I appointed you as a prophet to the nations."*[26] Jeremiah's relationship with God is interesting. In many theological circles, he is called the weeping prophet. There is an entire book in the Bible that he is penned as the author called the book of Lamentations. What does lamentations mean? It means weeping. Despite this, God gives him an encouraging word in Jeremiah 1:5 that speaks to divine relationship. Ladies and Gentlemen, this is the key, divine relationship, connection to your Source. This is how you are able to hear that voice. Let me close this case study by telling you a story about my daughter and I.

Our family would frequently get together to attend a community festival held by Union Temple Baptist church in Anacostia, Southeast Washington, D.C. There are thousands of people there. The music is blasting, people are everywhere. It is a cacophony of people, sounds and activity. In the midst of this, my wife, who was super vigilant with our children, for a split second, let go of my daughter's hand. In that split second, my daughter was gone! We looked everywhere and could not see or hear her. In a panic I yelled her name out, BIANCA!!! To my exhilaration I saw my little, vivacious, full of life daughter running toward me looking slightly confused and concerned. I grabbed her, hugged her, kissed her and then scolded her. "Don't you ever run off like that again!" I told her. She said, "But Daddy, they called and told all of the little children to come to the stage to get candy." I smiled and told her. "OK, please don't run off like that again." She never did. What is my point? There are a number of things you can draw from this, but I want to highlight three.

First, God is always speaking to us. Second, there will always be noise, distractions, voices calling you in a number of different directions. Third, and this is the most important, to hear the "still small voice" of God above all of the noise, you must have a familiarity with His voice.

You see, my daughter could distinguish my voice from

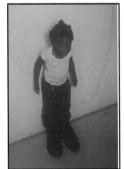 all the other voices for two reasons. She knew her name and she knew my voice. For all the things written in this book, that last sentence is the all important one. Know thy self and know the one who created you, because in doing so you will discover your gift, your purpose will be revealed to you and you will become the hero God called you to be.

Glossary

Averagarianism: A philosophy grounded in the mathematical concept that believes we can evaluate human beings through the use of one-dimensional factors in order to develop composite, ideal prototypical individual based on the average of those factors.

Bell Curve: A description used to describe a mathematical concept called normal distribution. In summary it aligns itself with any data that shows a trend where the most occurences happen in the middle of the distribution or mean, tapering off both in the beginning and ends of the distribution.

Dross: The impurities that separate from precious metals during the refining process as a result of intense heat being applied to the metal.

Frequency Illusion: A phenomenom in which an individual when they learn something new begin to see that new learned thing everywhere. Also called the Baader-Meinhof phenomenom.

Humility: The act of being mindful of your greatness while positioning yourself in a lower posture.

Imago Dei: A latin term that is used within theological circles especially in Catholicism. It reflects the theological thought that all human beings are created in the "Image of God", which is what Imago Dei translates.

Perverted You: This is a version of self that is the worst you can be. It is when you have allowed yourself to become distorted to the degree that you are the anithesis of who you were called to be.

Selective Attention: A thought process where an individual only pays attention to information that address or relate to needs or interests that align with that individual attitudes, opinons and beliefs

Success Awareness: The cognitive ability to be able to identify opportunities to succeed despite an environment that does not readily present them or even masks them.

Trinity of Gifting; The trinity of gifting is comprised of three components: Your Calling. Your Purpose. Your Gift.

True You: This is a form of self defined by an individual fully being exactly what they were created to be. It is a form of spiritual existentialism. It is when you completely know yourself and are in complete relationship with your Creator. It is your best self. It is completion of refinement.

YOU Spectrum: A range of you that spans from two aspects. On one end is the perverted you (see perverted you). On the other end is the true you (see true you).

Bibliography

Frankl, V. E. (n.d.). Man's Search for Meaning (Fourth Edition ed.). (I. Lasch, Trans.) Boston, MA: Beacon Press.

Frederick Winslow Taylor, M. S. (1913). The Principles of Scientific Management. New York, New York: Harper and Brothers Publisher.

Pressfield, S. (2002). The War of Art: Break Through the Blocks and Win Your Inner Creative Battles. New York, New York: Black Irish Entertainment, LLC.

QUETELET, A. (2013). TREATISE ON MAN AND THE DEVELOPMENT OF HIS FACULTIES. (T. Smibert, Ed., & R. Knox, Trans.) New York: Cambridge University Press.

Rohr, R. (2013). Immortal Diamond: the search for our true self (First ed.). San Francisco, CA: Jossey-Boss.

Rose, D. T. (2016). The End of Average: How to Succeed In A World That Values Sameness. New York, New York: HarperCollins.

Ross, L., Rouhani, P., & Fischer, K. W. (2013, August 16). The Science of the Individual. IMBES: Mind, Brain and Education, 7(3), pp. 152-158.

Sindell, G. (2009). The Genius Machine: The 11 Steps That Turn Raw Ideas Into Brilliance. Novato, California: New World Library.

Winnicott, D. W. (1965). The Maturational Process and the Facilitating Environment: Studies in the Theory of Emotional Development. New York, New York: International UP Inc.

Index

A

B

CPSIA information can be obtained
at www.ICGtesting.com
Printed in the USA
BVHW020833160820
586412BV00001B/1